MW01062358

Training
Kings & Queens

by Cindy Schaap

CHRISTIAN WOMANHOOD
CROWN POINT, INDIANA

ISBN: 0-9745195-7-X

All Scriptures used in this volume
are from the King James Bible.

Other Books by Cindy Schaap

A Wife's Purpose

Silk and Purple
Lessons for Wives and Mothers from Women in the Old Testament

A Meek and Quiet Spirit
Lessons for Wives and Mothers from Women in the New Testament

Living on the Bright Side
Principles for Lasting Joy, Especially for Ladies

The Fundamental Man
An Authorized Biography of Jack Frasure Hyles

From the Coal Mines to the Gold Mines
An Authorized Biography of Russell Anderson

Bright Side Planner/Journal

Printed and Bound in the United States

DEDICATION

This book is dedicated to my husband's and my children-in-love, Todd Weber and Candace Hooker Schaap. It is also dedicated to their parents, Ron and Marcia Weber and Bob and JoBeth Hooker. Without them, our child rearing could not have been complete. I would love to learn from them about parenting. In my opinion, they are experts on rearing kings and queens.

Todd & Jaclynn

Ken & Candace

Ron & Marcia Weber

Bob & JoBeth Hooker

ACKNOWLEDGMENTS

I would like to acknowledge my husband/pastor, Dr. Jack Schaap, for his encouragement to me in my writing and in all other aspects of my life. He is a wonderful pastor, husband, and father. I could not have had success in my child rearing without him.

I would like to thank my typesetter, Linda Stubblefield, for her invaluable work on all of the books I have written. She is an expert in her field. I would like to thank Jane Grafton, Rena Fish, and Rachel Wolfe for their help in proofreading.

I would like to thank my mother, Beverly Hyles, and my mother-in-law and father-in-law, Marlene and Ken Schaap, for their influence in my child rearing. They are the best! Many of the things I have written in this book I learned from them. Their influence has been invaluable.

I would like to acknowledge the memory of my three child-rearing mentors in Heaven: Dr. Jack Hyles, my father; my paternal grandmother, Coystal Hyles; and my baby sitter/alias adopted grandmother, Louise Clifton. The child in me still adores them all!

TABLE OF CONTENTS

FOREWORD

I t is impossible for me to put into words what an amazing lady my mother is. I asked her to write a child-rearing book because she is the perfect example of a mother, and I feel that if I can have the kind of relationship with my children that my mom had with me, then my children will feel loved and be successful.

As a mother, she loved and cared for us; as a teacher, she took the time to train us through love and discipline; as a friend, she had fun with us, laughed with us, cried with us, shared our victories as well as our defeats; as a role model, she is the best one I know; and I want to be just like her when I "grow up."

Mom, no one deserves to write a child-rearing book more than you do. You have been an outstanding example of a mother, and I hope we are and always will be a credit to your years of patience, training, and love. I love you.

– Jaclynn Weber

H ow do you define the perfect mother? What trait can you pick out about her in a few sentences that would explain her greatness? Mom wasn't just great during one stage of my life; she was a great mom through every stage that I went through. Mom was and is consistently great. She did her best at becoming everything a child could need from his mother.

Perhaps the greatest single thing my mom did for me was something that few people ever saw. Every morning I would walk down from my

11

bedroom, and I would see my mom on her knees praying in the living room. That image of her praying would stick with me throughout the rest of the day. Every decision I made was influenced by the thought of Mom's praying for me.

What else can I say? Mom made parenting look easy. I'm so glad she's sharing her wisdom in this book. This world would be an amazing place if there were a million mothers who worked as hard at parenting as Mom has.

– Ken Schaap

INTRODUCTION

I was driving our 25-year-old daughter Jaclynn to church recently, and she asked me when I was going to write a book on child rearing. I told her that I didn't know, and she asked me, "Could you at least have a book done by the time Lyndsay (Todd and Jaclynn's 19-month-old daughter) is a teenager?"

I must admit that I am excited and yet reluctant to write a book on this subject. I am excited because I am captivated by the subject of child rearing. I have enjoyed every stage of being a mother to Jaclynn and Kenny.

Forgive me for writing much of this book in first person. I write best this way, but I definitely do not want to appear to be a "know-it-all" in child rearing. I have read dozens and dozens of books on the subject. I believe that child rearing is one of the most ominous tasks known to mankind. No one is a perfect parent. I was not even close to perfect in my child rearing. I won't even know how I turned out until I die, much less knowing how our children turned out.

Sometimes it seems that wonderful parents turn out rebellious children and rebellious parents turn out wonderful children. The most definitive reason I can find for children's turning out right is the grace of a merciful God.

But children and grandchildren can get you to do things you wouldn't do otherwise. Therefore, I am writing this book at Jaclynn's request. I do believe strongly in the power of the written word. I believe in the unparalleled influence of passing on your beliefs to the next generation. Because of this, I am taking the risk of putting my thoughts on child rearing on paper for the next generation.

Though this book is not dedicated to Lyndsay and Raymond, our two grandchildren, they are in a roundabout way the reason why I am writing it. My prayer is that this book will be a help to all who read it and to all the grandchildren whom God sends to our family.

Perhaps the title *Training Kings and Queens* seems a bit presumptuous. I am not insinuating that we ought to rear our children to become royalty. Nor am I proposing that we rear our children to think they are better than others. The Bible teaches us that when a child is saved, he becomes a child of the King of Kings, our Lord Jesus Christ. The Bible also teaches that a child of God who does God's will on this earth will inherit rewards for eternity. This book is for the purpose of rearing that kind of king and that kind of queen.

Thank you for sharing this child-rearing book with me.

Cindy Schaap
Romans 4:20, 21

UNIT ONE

BABY CARE

1

THE EXPECTANT MOTHER

I don't remember ever NOT wanting to be a mother. I had dozens of baby dolls, and I played with them far beyond the normal age that girls play with dolls. I never was fond of the Barbie doll. It was the baby doll that captured my attention.

In July of 1980, several years after I had reluctantly packed away my baby dolls, I found that my husband of 15 months and I were expecting a real baby doll of our own. We both were terribly excited. The following are some things I believe we did right during the expectant years of our marriage:

1. We waited some time to start a family. The subject of birth control is one I try to avoid. It is, of course, very controversial. Though I am against some forms of birth control and believe that the birth control pill is dangerously overused, I don't believe it is always against God's will for a couple to plan when they will have children, no more than it is against God's will for them to set a wedding date or to decide how many years of college to take.

It is my extensive experience as a marriage counselor which leads me to believe in some type of family planning. Many times my husband must try to fix the problems in a marriage that we feel could easily have been avoided had the couple not had several children too soon and too close together.

My husband believes that the Bible teaches that the marriage relationship was established for the **primary** purpose of companionship and for the **secondary** purpose of reproduction. It is wise for a couple to

17

establish the companionship of their marriage before they establish their parenthood.

It is common for human nature to enjoy only the looking forward to the attaining of a relationship and then to fail to equally enjoy the relationship after it is in our possession. This faulty thinking can affect a marriage into the senior years. When our youngest child married recently, my husband and I had not lived alone for the 25 preceding years of our marriage.

My husband and I decided not to consider child bearing until after we had been married a full year. We took the time to enjoy that first glorious stage of newlywed life. We developed a friendship and a predictable rhythm in our marriage and in our finances our first year. I'm so glad that we did!

2. We did not wait too long to have a family. This statement seems contradictory to point one, but it is not. Many couples are waiting well into their twenties and thirties and some even into their forties before bearing children. These couples are establishing their careers and gaining financial status, while putting off starting a family.

I am thankful that my husband and I had our children at a young age. Many couples are suffering with infertility problems because of waiting too long to bear children. Other couples are finding themselves too old to enjoy or to keep up with the children and grandchildren. God made a woman's body to be its most fertile during her early twenties. This scientific fact alone should help us to understand God's thoughts on bearing children.

Though I do not believe the Bible teaches that reproduction is the **primary** reason for marriage, I do believe it is the **secondary** reason. A woman's secondary purpose for living is not to establish a career or to gain financial status.

3. We spaced our children a few years apart. When our first child Jaclynn was nine months old, I thought I was pregnant. I was very disappointed, not because I didn't want more children, but because I did not feel I had adequately established a relationship with our first child. As it turned out, I was not pregnant, and by the time our second child Kenny was born, I felt that I was completely ready.

I know that life cannot always go as planned and that each child should be very wanted regardless. God has a way of letting us know when His plans are not our plans, and He always knows best. However, it is wise for a couple to try to plan so that the wife's health is fully returned, the couple's marriage is firmly resettled, and the parents' relationship with the present child or children is firmly established.

As it turned out for us, my husband and I had only two children. After two high-risk childbirths, the doctor advised us against having any more. I do believe that *"children are an heritage of the Lord,"* and I admire people who have a quiver full of them. I never feel it is right to look down upon people who have a lot of children.

4.   I carefully followed proper nutrition during my pregnancies. Too many women forever lose their girlish figure during their first pregnancy by eating for two…or three…or four…or more. I ate a lot during my pregnancies, but I stayed away from sugar, white flour, caffeine and chemically processed foods. My weight gain was sufficient, but minimal; my babies were average-sized and healthy, and I quickly returned to my pre-pregnancy weight.

5.   I kept my husband involved with my pregnancy. From time to time, he would accompany me to the doctor. We did a lot of shopping and choosing for the baby together during those expectant months. I stayed active, and we continued having a weekly date night during my pregnancy, a habit we established right after we were married. I don't necessarily recommend this, but my husband and I went bowling the night before Jaclynn was born.

During pregnancy, it is easy for a woman to get in her own little world. She may eat, sleep, drink, and dream of nothing but the baby. The wise wife will always be bringing her husband into her world and taking herself into his. This is not the time for a woman to become disinterested or disconnected with her husband's jobs or interests.

It is not as easy for a man to become excited about what he cannot see. My husband did not talk much about the baby until we toured the hospital and took Lamaze classes. At the end of each class, he was so excited that he could hardly contain himself. The wise wife will find ways (especially visual ways) to keep her husband informed and interested in the pregnancy. My husband and I were fortunate enough to have a Christian Lamaze teacher come to our house and give private Lamaze classes to us and to one other couple. I am grateful to Carol Wing for her willingness to do this.

When our daughter Jaclynn and her husband Todd were expecting their first child, Pat Harrell, a former obstetric nurse who is now the nurse at our Hammond Baptist Schools, came to their house for private Lamaze classes, also. Todd and Jaclynn asked me to sit in on some of these classes, and Pat did a wonderful job!

6. I read a lot during my pregnancy. Most of my 25 years as a mother, I have been in the middle of a marriage or a child-rearing book. It always amazes me that doctors spend on the average of eight years studying to be a doctor, and many wives and mothers never crack open a book to study about their primary and secondary purposes for living.

7. I guarded my atmosphere while I was expecting Jaclynn and Kenny. I was one of those silly (?) expectant mothers who talked to her children while she was expecting! I also made sure to avoid stressful music and sounds for my coming baby. My husband and I tried harder than ever to avoid strife in our marriage.

On Thursday, April 16, 1981, our first child—a girl—was born. We gave her a love name. Her first name is Jaclynn, a combination of Jack (my husband's first name) and Lynn (my middle name). Her middle name is April, which is not only the month that she was born, but also the month my husband and I met and fell in love. Trendy names have come and gone during her 25 years of life, but her love name remains meaningful.

I went into the hospital with one goal in mind. I did not want to say anything to my husband that I would regret. My husband remained the central issue (my primary purpose), and he still is today. Our time together in the hospital was sweet. However, our baby's heartbeat went alarmingly low, and mine skyrocketed. Because of this, Jaclynn was taken by Caesarean section. The last words I heard the nurse say were, "Mr. Schaap, you had better put away your video camera. You won't be using it." My last thoughts were of concern for him, and his were for me.

Through God's miraculous intervention, a healthy baby was born in spite of the obstacles. I developed a serious infection and was unable to nurse our daughter at the beginning. My husband fed Jaclynn her first bottle and became her first nurturer.

On November 14, 1984, our son Kenneth Jack Frasure was born. Again, a love name was given. Kenneth is the name of my husband's father. Jack is both my husband's and my father's name. Frasure is the maiden name of my beloved paternal grandmother who passed away two months before Kenny's birth. I adored her, and Kenny never knew her.

With the birth of each child, the first stage of my parenting ended—the pregnancy stage. Though I have not been perfect in any stage of my life, I feel both pregnancies ended full of happiness. I had done my best to take care of my body and to prepare my soul for the experience of motherhood. Most of all, I started out doing for our children what would profit them the most. I loved their father. I did not forget that he was my primary purpose and my love for him was the very reason for their existence.

2

Postpartum Blues

There is a legitimate hormonal change that takes place a few days to a few weeks after childbirth that is referred to as postpartum blues. Every expectant mother should be aware of this hormonal change and should be prepared as to what to do.

I don't remember a specific instance of postpartum after our first was born, but after Kenny was born on November 14, 1984, I cried all during Thanksgiving dinner about ten days later. I didn't just ruin **my** Thanksgiving, but also the dinner of all those who were "privileged" to eat with me.

How to Prepare

1.   Decide ahead of time that if you feel any substantial amount of postpartum depression, you will call someone to get help. I warned our daughter to call me and not to allow herself to be alone if she felt this way after her pregnancies and after her miscarriage. Some postpartum sadness can be controlled by using practical principles that control the mind and spirit. However, some postpartum difficulty is indeed physical and should be expected.

I strongly urge you to resist any doctor's advice to take an antidepressant. Even the secular medical field is now voicing concern over how difficult it is to get off of antidepressants. I have also read secular books on nutrition written by medical doctors which claim many diseases can be caused by the use of antidepressants.

Natural progesterone or bioidentical may be a good choice to help with postpartum, but a nutritionist or preventive doctor should be consulted.

   2.   Put things back into your schedule according to your priorities and don't be too hard on yourself after the baby is born. The following are the priorities that I feel should be on every woman's list.

   A.   *Fellowship With God.* God made human beings to fellowship with Him.

   B.   *Husband.* God made the first woman to be a help to her husband.

   C.   *Children.* Woman's second highest calling is the rearing of her children.

   D.   *Soul Winning.* Soul winning is the only Christian ministry that God calls every Christian to do.

This doesn't mean that a new mother should scold herself if she doesn't read her Bible and pray the day after her baby is born. The new mother probably needs to just rest and care for her baby for a few days. But as soon as she is able, she should schedule her devotional time with God as a first add-in priority.

When Jaclynn was born, I cleaned the house pretty thoroughly the day after I arrived home from the hospital after having a Caesarean birth. Needless to say, I was young and naive. Some offered to help me during this time, but I turned down their help. As a whole, I believe I had a much more difficult time adjusting to Jaclynn's birth than to our second born.

When Kenny was born, I was a lot more lenient with myself regarding the house. Instead, I looked at my priority list and tried to add in things according to that list. We so often busy ourselves doing the less important things while the most important things suffer. I believe more good people mess up their lives and families over the matter of wrong priorities than over any other matter.

Two weeks after Kenny was born, I went on my regularly scheduled Friday night date with my husband. I left Kenny each Friday night thereafter with the same competent baby sitter. I also put Kenny in the nursery for soul winning on Friday morning two weeks after Kenny was born.

I scheduled in my Bible reading and prayer even before that.

My husband hired a house cleaner for me for six weeks after Kenny was born, and I took off six weeks from my part-time teaching job. I enjoy cleaning my own house and have never hired a house cleaner since, but I am thankful for the wisdom of my husband in providing this for me.

We often starve our marriages, our husbands, and our own souls at a time when these need the most reinforcement. **In doing this, we are too hard on ourselves, which is a key factor in postpartum depression.** We are also too hard on our husbands. I do not believe in neglecting one's husband sexually before or after childbirth. Obviously, some changes need to be made regarding intimacy, but the husband should not be neglected in this area altogether. I have done too much counseling to consider this an option. More than once I have seen a man lose his purity during his wife's postpartum. Though I do not see this man's sins as justified, I do believe a wife has a responsibility to protect her husband sexually to the best of her ability at all times. We also neglect Jesus during postpartum at a time when we need Him most. He has so much patience, wisdom, and comfort to give to the postpartum mother.

3. Live by the following acrostic in order to have joy during postpartum, as well as during any time of transition.

> J— JESUS
> O—OTHERS
> Y—YOURSELF

A. Spend extra time with Jesus during your recovery time and during baby's nap time.

B. Do something special for others during lonely times or times of transition. During postpartum, I would make most of your others time to be time spent for or with your husband and children.

C. Do something special for yourself. Pamper yourself a little bit. Read a good book, soak in a hot bath, go for a massage, and REST, REST, REST, REST! (I personally disfavor receiving a massage from the opposite gender, unless it is your spouse.)

Psalm 37:4, *"Delight thyself also in the LORD; and he shall give thee the desires of thine heart."* Psalm 37:4 says that we are to find our joy in the Lord. I have used this verse for many transitions in my life and have found that the Lord is more than enough to help us through any transitions in our lives.

Isaiah 40:11, *"He shall feed his flock like a shepherd: he shall gather the lambs with his arm, and carry them in his bosom, and shall gently lead those that are with young."*

UNIT TWO

TRAINING CHILDREN

REARING DISCIPLINED CHILDREN

One of the goals of every parent should be to rear a disciplined child. Too often we think the word "discipline" to be synonymous with the word "punishment" or "spanking." However, this is not the case. Allow me to illustrate.

Several years ago I was standing at a grocery store entrance helping our children sell candy bars. One of them was working for a trip to Washington, D.C. As a fundraiser for their grade school, it was promoted that the top 20 students who sold the most cases of candy bars could go on a five-day drip to Washington, D.C. To our disappointment, a father and son from another school came to the same door where we were already selling and began to sell candy bars also.

Not long after they started, the little son began to whine. I would guess the boy was about five years old. The father proceeded to tell his son to be quiet. The father was a very large man, and I felt sure that the boy would respond to his command to stop whining—but he continued to whine.

The exasperated father then told the little boy to "SHUT UP!"

The little boy continued whining.

The very angry father began to curse at the boy and yell, "SHUT UP, OR I'LL MAKE YOU SHUT UP!" I looked at the very big and angry father and thought, "If I were you, little boy, I would shut up. In fact, I'm very sure that I'm going to shut up." The little boy continued whining.

Finally, the irate father took off his belt and spanked the boy right at the grocery store doorway. But the little boy continued whining.

What is the moral of this story?

1. **You can't rear a disciplined child through anger.** It is my belief that the little boy in this story had been threatened, cursed at, and told to shut up before—so much so that he no longer feared those actions. He had become hardened to them.

2. **You can't rear a disciplined child through fear.** Dr. Don Boyd, the principal of Hammond Baptist High School, once said something like this, "If you rear a child to obey you because of fear, he will only obey you as long as he is afraid of you. If you rear a child to obey you because of love, he will obey the principles you have taught him for the rest of his life."

3. **You can't rear a disciplined child through punishment alone.** I am a firm believer in punishment as you will learn in this book. However, discipline includes much more than punishment.

The following is a list in order of what I consider to be the five steps to rearing a disciplined child.

1. PRAYER
2. LOVE
3. TEACHING
4. SCHEDULING
5. PUNISHMENT

All five are important and must be included to rear a disciplined child. None should be excluded. A child who is loved without punishment will become a spoiled child. A child who is punished without love will become a rebellious child such as the little boy mentioned above. When a child is not properly disciplined, a big strong man can lose the ability to control that child, usually even starting when the child is very little.

In the next chapters, we will discuss the five parts of disciplining children.

Part 1-Praying for Children

Pray as if everything depended on God,
and work as if everything depended on man.
–Spellman

INTRODUCTION

I believe prayer is the most important part of rearing a disciplined child. Why? Because God can do what we cannot do. I cannot tell you all of the reasons why a child turns out good or bad. As stated before, I believe the main reason that our children have prospered so far is that we have a merciful God Who has answered the prayers of two imperfect parents. I have failed our children in many ways, but I have saturated their lives in my prayers.

1

A Mother's Prayer for Her Children

I just finished mentally going through my prayer list and jotting down with pen and paper a list of things I pray for daily regarding our children. Allow me to share them with you:

1. Walk With God. I daily ask God to help them to read their Bible and pray that day, and I ask God to work in their lives that day.

2. Protection From the Devil and Sin. Each day I ask God to bind the Devil and to protect them from him and his works. I ask God to protect them from sin, temptation, the wrong crowd, the flesh, and the world as well.

3. Purity and Honesty. I ask the Lord each morning to keep my family pure and help them to be honest for the next 24 hours.

4. Protection From Harm. I ask Jesus each morning to keep my family alive, healthy, and safe for the next 24 hours. I ask Him to protect them from accidents. I ask Him to deliver them from anyone who might try to hurt them.

I know that should God allow anything to happen to my family, such as a serious illness, I will have added peace because I have prayed for them each day. I have also heard my children describe many near misses in their lives (especially when they were teenage drivers) when I silently thanked God for reminding me to pray for them that day.

5. Prosperity. Each morning I ask God to help my family to spend the day the way that He would want them to and to help them to prosper in whatever they do.

6. **Assurance of Salvation.** Each morning I ask God to give each family member assurance of their salvation for the next 24 hours. I also daily pray that our granddaughter Lyndsay will be saved as soon as she is old enough to understand her need for salvation.

7. **God's Perfect Will.** I pray daily that our children will do God's perfect will and that God will use them greatly. Being used greatly does not necessarily mean that I want them to accomplish some great feat that I have designed for them. Our son Ken recently had a part in the salvation of a teenage boy who said he was an atheist. That was great! Our daughter is having a yard sale to help pay for her Sunday school girl to go to a Christian school. That is part of the "greatly" I am talking about. Our daughter-in-law Candace recently wrote me of a young girl she had influenced at a camp where her tour group was singing. Todd, our son-in-law, quietly took a young boy in the youth group whose big brother was found dead the day before to lunch the other day. God answers my prayer and uses them daily and greatly.

8. **Their Marriages.** Each day I ask God to bless and to protect Todd and Jaclynn's marriage and Kenny and Candace's marriage. I ask God to help them to be good and loyal to each other.

9. **My Attitude.** Daily I ask God to help me not to worry unnecessarily or for wrong reasons over my children. I ask God to help my husband and me to stay close to our children without interfering with them.

10. **America.** Each day when I pray for America, I ask God to use my husband and me to help to preserve the freedom and safety of America. I always ask Him to help us to do it in order to repay the debt we owe our parents and for our children. Sometimes I grow tired of my husband's and my busy schedule. This prayer each morning motivates me more than almost anything:

> *Dear Jesus,*
>
> *Help us to do our part to preserve the freedom and safety of America for the next two generations—for Kenny, Candace, Todd, Jaclynn, and Lyndsay. Amen.*

I mention all of their names every morning, and somehow just saying their names keeps me going and helps me to encourage my husband.

I have really just summarized my prayers for our children. I am hoping that the above summary has given you some new ideas and/or motivation for praying for your children. Allow me to share three necessary items that should be a part of a mother's prayers and are a part of my prayers for Kenny (our son), Candace (our daughter-in-law), Jaclynn (our daughter), Todd (our son-in-law), and Lyndsay (our granddaughter).

- **Personalization.** In all of the praying I do for our children, I rarely use the words "our children." Rather I say, "Kenny, Candace, Todd, Jaclynn, and Lyndsay." Kenny dated Candace Hooker for over four years. By the time they married on December 17, 2005, I am sure I had prayed for her by name hundreds, maybe even thousands, of times. No wonder it is not hard for me to love our in-laws and to believe the best about them. I love Candace and Todd as if they were my own. I have prayed for Lyndsay in all of the same areas for which I pray for our children since the day she was born and for some requests since the day I heard she was expected.

- **Time.** My prayer list for our children is lengthy. Some days not all of the areas are covered. The majority of the time they are. Why? Because that is a large part of my job both as a mother and as a wife. I have been blessed to have a flexible enough schedule so that I can spend much time in prayer. If I had a busier job, I would have more worldly wealth, but would God be using my children? Many mothers have more time to pray because of the nature of their role. It is easier to pray at an ironing board than in a board room. Through prayer, more can be accomplished at an ironing board than in a board room.

- **Faith.** When I don't pray for my children as I should, it is easy for me to become uneasy. When I do pray for them as I should, nothing they do seems to rattle me. There is a part of me that honestly believes my family's world would fall apart without my prayers. Is this an arrogant statement? It doesn't make me feel arrogant. I know that others are praying for them, probably just as diligently. But this kind of attitude not only motivates me to keep praying, but it also has helped me to see some awesome answers to prayer in my life.

I watch my children daily to be sure I don't miss praying for a need of theirs. One day a couple of years ago, I made notes of specific requests I had recently been praying for our children. Kenny was taking Greek in summer school, and I asked God to help Kenny learn Greek. I asked God to help the junior high activity that Todd and Jaclynn were on that day to go well. (Todd is the junior high youth director at First Baptist Church of Hammond.) I asked that Lyndsay would do well with the baby sitter. I prayed for grace for Candace as she and Kenny were apart from each other much of that summer.

Sometimes my children will ask me to pray for them about a particular matter. Usually I can honestly say I have already been praying about it. I might teasingly say, "You know your mother. I try to cover all the bases with my prayers."

More than once they have walked away with a grin and said simply, "Mother and her prayers." They seemed happy, and therefore, as a mother, so was I.

2

PRAYING FOR YOUR CHILDREN

Mathew 15:21-28; Mark 7:24-30

In Matthew 15:21-28 and again in Mark 7:24-30, an account is given about a woman who came to Jesus, falling at His feet and asking for healing for her demon-possessed daughter. This is a story in the Bible of a parent praying for her child's spiritual welfare, and many lessons can be learned in this story about how a mother should pray for her child. Allow me to share them with you.

1. In order to pray for her child properly, a mother should recognize her enemy. Some readers may not believe that this story applies to them and to their child because the daughter in this story was demon-possessed. Now believe me, I am **not** trying to insinuate that your children or mine are demon-possessed—though I have seen some who acted like it, especially two year olds.

However, it is the Devil who is our child's enemy. Our enemy is not really the wrong crowd. The enemy is not even rock music or drugs. Our enemy is the Devil, the worldly system which he controls, and the flesh of our children which the Devil would **like** to control.

This is why each morning, usually in the early morning hours, I pray and ask God to bind the Devil and not to allow him to have any power or authority upon my children's lives. Probably my children will be tempted—even Jesus was tempted. But I believe the Syrophenician woman is an example to us, in teaching us that we ought to pray a hedge of protection from the Devil around our children.

Parents also need to remember that their children's leaders are not their enemy. Sometimes a well-meaning Christian school teacher or youth director may make a decision which seems to be hindering rather than helping a mother to rear her child. Still that mother should support rather than fight those leaders. She should realize that it is the Devil who tries to divide the different authorities in our children's lives. He is the one we should fight, and prayer is our most powerful weapon against him.

2. **In order to pray for her child properly, a mother should pray humbly.** Jesus loved the Syrophenician woman even though He was a Jew and this woman was a Greek who was looked down upon by the Jews. When the disciples asked Jesus to send this woman away, Jesus responded to them by asking them to send for her.

But Jesus' response **to** this woman was very different. He called the Syrophenician woman a dog. Mark 7:27 tells us, *"But Jesus said unto her, Let the children first be filled: for it is not meet to take the children's bread, and to cast it unto the dogs."* Jesus was saying that His favored children (the Jews) should receive His miracle and blessing and not the Gentiles of which she was a part.

There is an old saying which reads, "Sticks and stones may break my bones, but words can never harm me." While I believe this saying to be true, I still would feel "harmed" if my Saviour called me a dog. (Come to think of it, being a Gentile, I guess He did!)

The Syrophenician woman responded humbly. Mark 7:28, *"And she answered and said unto him, Yes, Lord: yet the dogs under the table eat of the children's crumbs."* She responded by saying, "Yes, Lord. Yes, I am a dog." This mother was humble as she prayed for her daughter.

For many years, I prayed to the Lord for my children by saying things like this:

Dear Lord, You know I have tried hard to be a good mother. You know how hard I work to do what You want me to do. Please help my children to turn out right.

This, I believe is a wrong way to pray. I was proud in my prayers and trying to impress God with my parenting skills which, by the way, I could never do. Since studying the life of the Syrophenician woman, my prayers are more like this:

> *Dear Lord, be merciful to me a sinner. I know I could never be all a mother should be, but I trust Your mercy, and I ask You to protect my children from the Devil and help them to turn out right.*

In other words, I used to pray more like the Pharisees, but I am learning to pray more like the sinner that I am.

Another thing which I think helps me to pray more humbly is having a scheduled time each week when I call out many, many names of the children of my friends and of my peers in the ministry to the Lord. My prayer for my children to turn out right is not a prayer to impress others with my mothering skills. Neither is it a prayer which I hope will guarantee that my children turn out better than anyone else's children. I am pulling for my children, and I am pulling for the children of others.

3.   In order to pray for her child properly, a mother should pray in faith. The Syrophenician woman demonstrated her faith in three ways through her prayer.

First of all, when God hurt her feelings and did something which she may have found hard to understand, she said, "Yes, Lord." She agreed with God.

Many parents do not see their prayers answered for their children because they are in disagreement with God. God allows something to happen in their lives which hurts them. Perhaps they or someone they love becomes seriously ill. Perhaps another person hurts them, perhaps even a preacher. They become bitter against God, and in their bitterness, God does not answer their prayers. They lose their children because of an ugly thing like bitterness.

Parents often fail to realize that their best opportunity to transfer their faith in Jesus and to prove His superiority over what the Devil has to offer is when trials come. Some of the worst children I have ever met are preachers' kids. However, some of the best children I have ever met are the children of a pastor and his wife who have been through a church split. Why? I believe it is because they have had the opportunity to watch their parents go through trials and have seen them say without bitterness, "Yes, Lord."

I have had the opportunity to see my parents go through situations where God might have seemed to be unkind, and I have seen the response of my parents. They have said, "Yes, Lord. Whatever God does is best, and God is always good." I am grateful for their example in this way. It has helped to transfer their faith to me and to make me more what I ought to be for God.

Secondly, the Syrophenician woman displayed her faith by believing that God had something for her. She said, "…*yet the dogs under the table eat of the children's crumbs.*" This mother humbly recognized her own weaknesses, yet she still believed that God wanted to answer her prayer and that God had a miracle for her.

It is sometimes difficult for me to have faith that my children could be used of God with a mother like me…but then I remember the Syrophenician woman, and I tell God that I believe that He will answer my prayers. I believe that God wants us to take the time each day not only to ask for things, but also to express our faith in Him. He wants us to brag on Him and to express to Him our belief in what He can do for our children.

Thirdly, this mother displayed her faith by continuing to seek Jesus when others tried to turn her away. The disciples tried to stop her from seeing Jesus. But she pressed on for her daughter's sake! When others don't believe in you or in your children, keep praying. When others would discourage you from seeking Jesus' face about something, when they would try to convince you the situation is hopeless, keep on praying.

Jesus Himself seemed to hesitate to answer her prayer. But she pressed on! Her daughter was far away from her presence. But she pressed on! What an encouragement to the parents of wayward children, who may not even know where their child is.

When the woman finished her plea to Jesus, He answered her prayer. Mark 7:29, "*And he said unto her, For this saying go thy way; the devil is gone out of thy daughter.*" Jesus answered her prayer because of what she said. Surely then we would want to learn what she said. Again, her statement was, *"...Yes, Lord: yet the dogs under the table eat of the children's crumbs."*

She responded with humility, and she responded with faith. *"And when she was come to her house, she found the devil gone out, and her daughter laid upon the bed."* (Mark 7:30) Jesus answered this mother's prayer for her daughter. It is with humility and with faith that we also can see our prayers answered for our children.

Lord, I believe that You can give our children protection from the Devil and that You can use them and make them all that You would have them to be. I ask You to do exactly that for my children and for the children of others. Amen.

3

PRAYING FOR CHILDREN

"And when he came to his disciples, he saw a great multitude about them, and the scribes questioning with them. And straightway all the people, when they beheld him, were greatly amazed, and running to him saluted him.

And he asked the scribes, What question ye with them? And one of the multitude answered and said, Master, I have brought unto thee my son, which hath a dumb spirit; And wheresoever he taketh him, he teareth him: and he foameth, and gnasheth with his teeth, and pineth away: and I spake to thy disciples that they should cast him out; and they could not.

He answereth him, and saith, O faithless generation, how long shall I be with you? how long shall I suffer you? bring him unto me. And they brought him unto him: and when he saw him, straightway the spirit tare him; and he fell on the ground, and wallowed foaming. And he asked his father, How long is it ago since this came unto him?

And he said, Of a child. And ofttimes it hath cast him into the fire, and into the waters, to destroy him: but if thou canst do any thing, have compassion on us, and help us. Jesus said unto him, If thou canst believe, all things are possible to him that believeth.

And straightway the father of the child cried out, and said with tears, Lord, I believe; help thou mine unbelief. When Jesus saw that the people came running together, he rebuked the foul spirit, saying unto him, Thou dumb and deaf spirit, I charge thee, come out of him, and enter no more into him.

And the spirit cried, and rent him sore, and came out of him: and he was as one dead; insomuch that many said, He is dead. But Jesus took him by the

42

hand, and lifted him up; and he arose. And when he was come into the house, his disciples asked him privately, Why could not we cast him out? And he said unto them, This kind can come forth by nothing, but by prayer and fasting." (Mark 9:14-29)

This passage in Mark provides additional information on praying for children. As Jesus was speaking to the multitudes, one man told Jesus of his son who had a deaf and dumb spirit. This spirit was causing the son to throw himself into dangerous situations such as fire and deep water. This can be compared to the behavior of those in our generation who struggle with drug addictions, alcoholism, manic depression, and so forth. In reality, any sin is rooted in the Devil and his kingdom and carries with it some degree of insanity.

1. **Bring your child and his problems to Jesus in prayer.** *"And one of the multitude answered and said, Master, I have brought unto thee my son, which hath a dumb spirit; He answered him, and saith, O faithless generation, how long shall I be with you? How long shall I suffer you? bring him unto me. And they brought him unto him: and when he saw him, straightway the spirit tare him; and he fell on the ground, and wallowed foaming."* (Mark 9:17, 19, 20) The first step that this heartbroken father took was the right step. He brought his son to Jesus. Though this father was able to talk to Jesus in person, we are no less bringing our children and their problems to Jesus when we talk to Him in prayer.

Our 22-year-old son Kenny went through some struggles with wrong music when he was 15. He shared with me in a letter last year that even when he was in his deepest struggles, he was convicted because he knew I was probably praying for him at that very moment.

2. **Ask for Jesus' help and compassion.** *"And ofttimes it hath cast him into the fire, and into the waters, to destroy him: but if thou canst do any thing, have compassion on us, and help us."* (Mark 9:22) Here is another illustration of how humbly we should ask for God's help. Notice this father did not give Jesus his list of credentials as a father. Rather he begged for Jesus' compassion.

Compassion is feeling someone else's hurt to the point that you are moved to action. A parent fails to rear good children when he tries to rely on his own efforts too much. Instead, he should be begging for God to get involved and to **do** something to help his child. We should involve God in every part of our children's lives through prayer, whether it be the terrible twos, potty training, or teenage rebellion. God should be consulted in **everything**!

    3. Have faith. *"Jesus said unto him, If thou canst believe, all things are possible to him that believeth."* (Mark 9:23) Jesus gave an immediate answer to the troubled father. It is always good to take note of Jesus' immediate answers. Jesus immediately exhorted this dad to believe. Though we should have confidence as parents, faith is not always having perfect confidence. Faith is continuing to seek God for your child when things are going wrong and it doesn't seem like prayer is working. It is also continuing to obey God's principles for child rearing, even when it seems that **they** might not be working.

    We should not rear our children out of fear; fear causes us to over-react to our children's problems. We should rear our children in faith. We should believe that our children are going to turn out right.

    4. Tell God you believe your children will turn out right. *"Lord, I believe; help thou mine unbelief."* (Mark 9:24b) Praying for our children to continue to turn out right is a part of my daily prayer list. It is also a ritual of mine to tell God afterwards that I **believe** our children will turn out right. Why do I do this? Because I have noticed that most of the time when God worked a miracle and answered a prayer for someone in the New Testament, it was right after that person said to Jesus, "I believe."

    5. Ask God to strengthen your faith that your children will turn out right. *"Lord, I believe; help thou mine unbelief."* (Mark 9:24b) I love the humanity of this statement. I not only tell God often that I believe He will answer my prayers, but I also ask Him often to help my unbelief. All prayers are mixed with faith and doubt. Faith is continuing to pray when you are filled with doubt.

    6. Cry for your child. *"And straightway the father of the child cried out, and said with tears, Lord I believe…."* (Mark 9:24a) Ask God to give you tears for your child. Most of that crying should not be in front of your child, to get your child's attention. Rather it should before God to get God's attention.

7. Fast. *"And he said unto them, This kind can come forth by nothing, but by prayer and fasting."* (Mark 9:29) I am no great hero of the faith who fasts for 40 days and nights, but I have fasted many times for 24 hours for our children.

Notice that things got worse before they got better. Jesus dealt with the sin and brought the child to a near-death situation. The father had to keep believing and praying during this time. Acting upon the father's request, his belief, and his tears, God revived the life of this man's son.

CONCLUSION

Without a doubt, I believe prayer to be the number one step to rearing a king or a queen. With the Devil, the flesh, and a world growing more and more wicked fighting against us, we can only rear a good child through the supernatural power of God.

I have made many mistakes as a parent; there are no perfect parents. The only reason that my children have turned out right or that any child turns out right is the mercy of a loving God.

PART II–LOVING CHILDREN

If there is anything better than to be loved,
it is loving.
–Anonymous

1

LOVE IS THE KEY

Recently, I was having my car worked on and was using my husband's car for a few days. At one point, I mistakenly tried to start my car with the key that belonged to my husband's car. I must admit I was rather frustrated when I realized that I would have to leave the garage and go back into the house to get the right key. Not just a key, but the right key had to be used to get my husband's car to obey me. Until the right key was used, the car acted in disobedience to my desires. Once the right key was found and used, the car followed my every command. So it is with child rearing.

Love is the key that unlocks the heart of a child. Once a child has given his heart away to his parents, the parent will easily be able to lead that child in the ways of the Lord. This principle is taught in the Bible. Proverbs 23:26, "*My son, give me thine heart, and let thine eyes observe my ways.*" When a parent has the heart of his child, that child will want to observe and follow the ways of the parent.

When I was a little girl, I was sitting on my father's lap, and I saw tears running down his cheek. In talking to him, I realized my daddy was crying for a hurt that I had; his concern and his tears were for me. I remember it like it was yesterday. That day a part of my heart left my body and was given to my daddy. I was the stereotypical "Daddy's girl." It was always easy to obey Dad, even during my teenage years. I strived to pass on his "ways" as I reared our own two children. Even though my dad has been in Heaven now for five years and I am no longer a little girl but a 46-year-old woman, I still think often of my dad's ways and find myself following them. In numerous ways, my father won my heart with his love. I, in turn, observed his life and tried to implement his principles into my own life. Love is the key that Dad used to capture my heart.

Not just any key will work, however. It must be the right key to start the car. A key for a Toyota will not do anything for a Ford car and vice versa. Not just any love key will jump start the heart of a child. It must be the love key which is appropriate for the age and personality of that individual child.

The Bible teaches us that **love is an action.** It is not just a statement or a feeling. I John 3:18 says, *"My little children, let us not love in word, neither in tongue; but in deed and in truth."*

If we love someone, we must do something about it, or that love will die. It will not remain just a feeling in our hearts.

If we love someone, we must not only do something about it; we must do something to which our loved one relates. My dad taught me that the word "relate" is one of the most important words for rearing teenagers.

When our son Kenny was four years old, my husband and I went on a Bahamian cruise to celebrate our tenth wedding anniversary. We left our children with grandparents for the week. "Mom," Kenny said before we left, "when you come back, I want you to wear the white dress with the red flowers and give me 40 hugs and 40 kisses." As the mother of a four year old, it was easy to comply. I did indeed wear the white dress with the red flowers and gave Kenny 40 hugs and 40 kisses…and I do believe that Kenny felt loved.

However, when Kenny was a teenager, I do not feel that giving him 40 hugs and kisses would have made him feel loved. He might would have rather been run over by a Mac truck! I did kiss and hug our teenage son from time to time. But that was not the primary key I used to make him feel loved. Instead, I used keys to which he could better relate. I watched football games with him; I chaperoned dates; I went to all of his basketball games.

Now as the mother of a married son, I realize the key has changed once again. I still kiss and hug Ken from time to time, but most of his hugging and kissing is needed from his wife. He doesn't really need me to watch football games with him, though I may do this from time to time. Kenny needs me to love his wife Candace. She is now the key.

Many a teenager and adult has parents who love him, but he does not feel loved. Why? Because the parent wants to express his love with the key that they became comfortable using when their offspring was a child. Parents should not make themselves the issue by loving their children in the way the parent wants, but rather in the way the child wants and relates to.

Charles Spurgeon used to say, "I want to so live so that when I look up to Heaven and say, 'I love you, Jesus,' Jesus can look down and say, 'I know it, Charles.' "

To this thought I would like to say "Amen" and then add, "I want to so live that when I look at our children and say, 'I love you,' they can look back and say, 'I know it, Mom.' "

One of the best books I have ever read on child rearing is *How to Really Love Your Child* by Dr. Donald Ross Campbell (Victor Books, Wheaton, Illinois, 1977). In this book Dr. Campbell gives four ways to show love so that a child will know he is loved. Actually, I think these four ways are universal and relate to people of all ages:

- Focused Attention
- Eye Contact
- Touch
- Praise

1. Focused attention. Focused attention is the time spent with an individual person doing something that he/she enjoys. I enjoy times when the whole family gets together, but I have always made it a point to have one-on-one time with each family member.

When our children were babies, I had a scheduled rocking chair and singing time with them a couple of times a day. As they became active toddlers and not as cuddly, I would sit them on their changing table and sing to them. I would try to make the singing time so much fun by acting out the songs that they didn't mind sitting still. I also began reading simple books to them.

When Jaclynn and Kenny were preschool and grade school age, I had a scheduled time when I let them pick out an activity to do with me. Jaclynn sometimes chose having a beauty contest with her dolls, but her favorite thing was just to cuddle on the couch and read. This made me very happy because I have a natural bent to find fun in couch-potato reading myself.

Kenny, however, did not relate as well to couch-potato reading. He usually chose something different, like playing cars or playing baseball. Kenny had a lot of metal cars, and he loved to make them crash with each other. Oftentimes, my fingers got in the way of a metal car crash. I can honestly say that I have been hurt several times in many car accidents. Fortunately, none of them ever sent me to the hospital.

Many afternoons when Kenny was small, I spent part of my afternoon running bases in our side yard. I remember occasionally saying to myself, "For this I got my college degree." Kenny is married now, however. When I return home from work today, the house will be empty. Now that my baseball days with Kenny are over, I take great comfort in the fact that I enjoyed every second that I played with Kenny. I have no regrets.

When our children had Christmas vacation from school, I anticipated their being home by planning one special activity for each day that they were home. One day we might bake cookies and take them to a neighbor; one day we might watch a Christmas video I had purchased; one day we might make a craft I had planned. Jaclynn, now a piano teacher, recently shared with me how several of her piano students said they were bored at home during Christmas vacation. "Mom," Jaclynn shared, "I don't remember ever being bored at home." And she never was. I viewed having a day home with our children as a precious gift and made it an exciting adventure.

I remember one snowed-in day tying our yellow Labrador Retriever to a sled. Jaclynn, Kenny and I took turns sledding down the street. (We live on a very quiet street, I might add.) This was not an activity that sounded fun to me until I talked myself into it and got involved in it. It turned out to be great fun, and coming in to hot chocolate and a lot of laughter was even more fun. None of us were bored or lonely or felt unloved that day, even though my husband was gone preaching out of town.

As our children became teenagers, we played many board games together. Jaclynn and Kenny also became much busier as teenagers. Because of this, I had to rearrange and slow down my schedule so that I could be at all of their school events. I don't recall missing any time that they sang in a singing group or participated in a cheerleading or an athletic event.

I promised myself when our two children were babies that I would never let 24 hours pass without spending individual time with them. I recall one evening realizing that I had not had any one-on-one time with our teenage daughter. While she was taking a bath, I asked her if she could close the curtain and I could come in. I sat on the floor and talked to Jaclynn about her day. A few weeks later Jaclynn commented that she didn't know of any other mother who would have taken the time to sit on the floor and talk to her daughter during her bath. This simple gesture, which took only a short time, seemed to speak volumes to Jaclynn.

I counsel mothers of larger families to make a vow to spend one-on-one time with each child every week instead of every day.

Now that our children are adults, my husband, who is a busy pastor, and I still give them individual attention. In fact, our daughter is meeting my husband for lunch on the very day I am writing this portion of this book. All of our family has a traditional roast beef dinner together at our house every Sunday afternoon. Every other Tuesday we also have a family night at one of our houses.

Every other Friday I have a breakfast or lunch date with either Jaclynn or Candace or with both of them. I baby-sit Lyndsay, our grand-daughter, every Saturday morning. I may end up baby-sitting her at other times, but Saturday morning is our special time when I do nothing but play with and care for Lyndsay.

2. **Touch.** In a college class, a visiting speaker fielded questions for a while. The speaker was Mrs. Lloys Rice, the wife of a well-known evangelist who had reared six lovely daughters, all serving the Lord. One of the questions asked of her was this: "What is the key to rearing good children?" There is that "key" word again. Though there is not just one key to rearing good children, the wise person is always searching for

one. My ears perked up to hear the answer to this question.

Mrs. Rice was such a godly lady; I was just sure her answer would be spiritually profound. Maybe she read 100 Bible verses a day to each girl. Instead, I found Mrs. Rice's answer to be profoundly simple. She said the word "stroke" is the key to rearing good children. She explained a stroke to be a nonsexual (of course) TOUCH that is used to show love to a child. We all need to be touched.

My husband and I rarely pass each other at home without touching. I strive to hug our children whenever I see them, even though they are all adults. I give lots of hugs and kisses on chubby cheeks to our granddaughter. I can see that she is learning the importance of touch also. Lately, every time I pick her up, Lyndsay begins to pat me over and over on the shoulder. I return the affection by patting her little arm. Lyndsay doesn't know the words "I love you" yet, but I do believe she knows that she is loved.

3. **Eye contact.** It has been said that even tiny babies crave EYE CONTACT. From early on, they look for another pair of eyes to set their own eyes upon. One of the earliest signs of growth and intelligence is seen when a parent notices his baby looking for eyes.

Eye contact is something that is most definitely displayed between couples who are dating. Sadly, it is one of the most neglected methods of showing love between married couples.

Busy mothers often show their frustration with misbehaving children by refusing to meet their eyes. One of the primary reasons that children misbehave is to get attention. If they misbehave long enough, perhaps Mom will grab their cheeks and say with agitation, "LOOK AT ME!" It may have been negative attention, but as soon as the eye contact is made between mother and child, the child realizes that he has found a way to get attention.

The wise mother will get on her knees from time to time when her child is being good and will look that child in the eyes. "I'm so proud of you. You are being such a good girl," she should say. This kind of attention, along with proper eye contact, will eliminate much negative behavior on the part of the child.

4. **Praise.** If I could give one word to describe how to have healthy

relationships, be it a marriage relationship, a parent-child relationship or any other, that one word would be "praise." *"As the fining pot for silver, and the furnace for gold; so is a man to his praise."* (Proverbs 27:21) Praise creates a picture of what our loved ones can become, and they begin to act out that praise. The same response comes from criticism. In my marriage, I have tried to live by these two rules:

- Never say anything negative about my husband.
- Take every opportunity to say something positive about my husband.

Though I am far from fitting the description of the virtuous woman in Proverbs 31, these rules remind me of Proverbs 31:26, *"She openeth her mouth with wisdom; and in her tongue is the law of kindness."*

The same rules have been applied to my children. Many people who would never think of criticizing their boss or their neighbor have no trouble laughing and discussing the negative traits of their children.

It is good to praise our children **directly**. We ought to tell them specifically and frequently what we admire and like about them. We ought to praise our children **indirectly**. I am not talking about bragging on and on about our children to others. I try to keep in mind that other people's children are just as special to them as mine are to me. However, I do try to plant positive seeds about my loved ones so that they will hear from others how proud of them I am. Hearing something nice said about you behind your back reaches the heart more effectively than even direct praise. Indirect praise does not go in one ear and out the other. It goes in the ears and reaches the heart. It is a great way to say to your child, "I love you," and to have them respond, "I know you do!"

When I was a little girl about eight years of age, I wrote a story and gave it to my father. After reading it, he dictated a letter to his secretary, and she typed it. I felt like such a big girl receiving this typewritten letter from my father. In the letter, my dad told me how much he liked my story, not only because I wrote it, but also because it showed him that I thought deeply and wrote my thoughts on paper. I can't imagine that this story written by an eight year old was really all that deep. But from that point on, I strove to think deeply and to write my thoughts on paper. My dad painted a picture for me, and I began to act it out. It is no wonder that I am an author, now writing my seventh book, and the most ironic thing is that I became my father's biographer. In 1998 I wrote a 528-page biography about my dad's life.

When I was a teenager, my dad often commented to me how deeply I thought and how he loved to talk to me because I loved to philosophize. He also commented about how much he loved to be around me because I loved so deeply. He bragged on the rest of my family too, yet he found unique ways to make me feel like I was special. I have two sisters who play the piano beautifully. I took piano lessons for five years and never caught on to it, but my dad's praise helped me to retain my confidence even though I did not always feel as talented or as beautiful as my two older sisters. My mother-in-law, Marlene Schaap, is another person in my life who I believe is an expert on giving praise.

Though I believe that Dr. Campbell's list is much greater than mine, I added my own two love conveyers: **gentleness** and **interest**.

5. Gentleness. When I am irritated or rushed, I lose my GENTLENESS. The abrupt, harsh treatment by an angry or busied parent wounds the spirit of a child and causes him to feel unloved. What can heal this wounded spirit? It is gentleness. As a parent, when I felt that I had wounded our children's spirits, and unfortunately, sometimes it happened, I would get down on my knees and look them in the eye. I would soften my voice and touch them gently. I would say "I am sorry," and I would begin to take the steps of focused attention, appropriate touch, eye contact, and praise to begin to heal their spirits.

6. Interest. Another effective method for conveying love, especially to a teenager, is INTEREST. Love is being interested in what your loved one is interested in, even if it does not come naturally for you.

My paternal grandmother, Coystal Hyles, lived to a few months before her ninety-seventh birthday. All of the years that I knew her, Mamaw, as I called her, was vital in my life though I could hardly call her beautiful at the age of 96. She was extremely wrinkled, small, and frail. She wore thick "Coke-bottle" glasses and still could barely see. She was hard-of-hearing, but I loved to be around her. Why? Because she was interested in what I was interested in. She was interested in **me**.

My grandmother was not able to spend much time with my husband. She did not get to know him very well. But whenever I was around Mamaw, she bragged excessively about my husband to me. Mamaw loved Jack Schaap dearly. She did not love him for any other reason than that I loved him. That was the way Mamaw was. When I would go to see Mamaw, she always insisted on sitting as close to me on the couch as she possibly could. She would hold my hand the entire time. Though she never heard my husband preach, she often bragged on his preaching. She repeated good comments she had heard from others. She would brag on me and would talk to me about my interests. I felt very loved by my grandmother.

SIX WAYS TO SHOW LOVE SO THAT ALL CAN FEEL LOVED

1. Focused Attention
2. Eye Contact
3. Touch
4. Praise
5. Gentleness
6. Interest

2

Providing a Good Environment

P roviding a good environment is also a vital key in child rearing. Before I married my husband, I asked him to describe what he wanted our home to be. He answered in one word, "Happy." Environment alone cannot express love to a child. Praise, focused attention, touch, eye contact, gentleness, and interest are the primary keys for expressing love. However, two secondary keys in expressing love to children are environment and money.

Many parents make the mistake of providing the secondary keys for showing love while neglecting the primary keys. Others fail at providing the secondary keys.

Some busy parents throw money and extravagant gifts at their children in order to make up for their lack of time and interest. These parents need to learn that while lack of financial provision is a great way to portray a lack of love, substituting money for time is also.

Warm, nutritious meals are important. A wise mother will study nutrition and will be disciplined in her own eating so as to help her children in this area. I have read that 90 percent of all ear infections are caused by sugar. Things like restricting sugar, artificial sweeteners, and chemically processed foods can do so much to enhance a child's behavior and personality, as well as his health.

Clean and pressed laundry and a clean house are also vital keys in child rearing, although we must remember that they are secondary and not primary methods for expressing love. It is of great importance that we as parents provide our children with an environment where they can feel loved.

The following are some ideas about how to make the environment of your home a happy one.

1. Play beautiful music. Before my husband became a pastor, he was a bus captain. He was in charge of a bus and a group of workers who brought children to Sunday school whose parents did not come. His bus route was in a poor, gang-infested area. From time to time, our family would host one of my husband's bus children for our traditional Sunday dinner, which usually consists of roast beef, potatoes and gravy, green beans, rolls, and dessert. (I only served dessert on Sundays.)

One little girl returned home after visiting our home one Sunday and proclaimed, "The Schaaps are rich; they play music when they eat!" Playing music during Sunday dinner was a tradition when our children were small, and it actually costs very little. I have never forgotten this story and have used it to remind myself how important the little touches are to a child's environment. It can be the small touches that make a poor- or middle-class family seem like a rich family. My husband and I still play beautiful music as we get ready for church on Sunday morning, as we get ready for bed in the evenings, and on holidays.

2. Light candles. I light candles for special occasions and for Sunday dinners. As just a small boy, our son said to me one Sunday, "Mom, you forgot to light the candles, and it's Sunday. Would you like me to light them for you?" I was surprised that the lighting of candles meant so much to our son, and I made myself a promise to never forget to light the candles.

3. Decorate for holidays. Most of my storage area in my basement is filled with decorations for Valentine's Day, Easter, Spring, Fourth of July, Fall, Thanksgiving, and Christmas.

4. Pray for the peace of your home. Jeremiah 29:7, *"And seek the peace of the city whither I have caused you to be carried away captives, and pray unto the LORD for it: **for in the peace thereof shall ye have peace."***

Surely if God wanted the Israelites to pray for the peace of the city in which they were slaves, He would want us to pray for the peace of our homes. God knows that if we bring peace to our environments, we are bringing peace to ourselves.

The Devil is constantly trying to bring strife to our lives, our homes, and our relationships. I Peter 5:8, 9 says, *"Be sober, be vigilant; because your adversary the devil, as a roaring lion, walketh about, seeking whom he may devour."* We must pray for the peace of our homes.

5. Bring a sense of order to your home. I have a certain way that I do things in my home. I have a place for everything and everything in its place. I like my home to be in a certain way when I return, so that I can feel peaceful. I know that an orderly environment makes a peaceful wife and mother, and a peaceful wife and mother makes for a happy family.

When my family is home, I do not pick up after them much. When they are gone, I have a scheduled time each day when I return our home to its previous state of order.

6. Don't bring things into your home which would not be happy and peaceful. Most of what is on the radio and television is not peaceful. Today's talk shows love to display strife between family members. The court shows which are so popular today are filled with strife. Soap operas are based on two themes: sex and anger.

7. Keep the candy jar filled in your home. I usually put out a candy jar in our house for each holiday. Our son-in-law Todd commented about how much he loves it that I do that and how his mother, Marcia Weber, has always done that also. I really don't eat much candy; I keep a filled candy jar because I realize it is the small touches that make a home feel festive and happy.

I am concluding this chapter with an article by Mrs. Leslie Beaman about one of my heroines who is now in Heaven, Mrs. Marlene Evans. I think it profoundly and eloquently expresses how I feel about providing a happy environment for our children.

The Candy Jar Is Empty
by Leslie Beaman

A few years ago my mother passed away. I went to visit my father three weeks after my mother's funeral, and I brought my two sons with me. My younger son always approaches life with a very logical, analytical view. He was very young at the time of this visit, but I'll never forget his first comments. When walking into my parents' living room, my son Adam said, "The music isn't playing, the candles aren't burning, the candy jar is empty—Grandma's dead." My mother was definitely the color in our home.

Mrs. Marlene Evans was and always will be one of the most colorful people I've ever known. A visit to her house meant the sight of a burning fireplace, the smell of Yankee candles burning, and the sounds of music playing. She really loved the sound of the piano and, of course, visits to the best restaurant in town. Mrs. Evans always wore "Beautiful" perfume, and to this day, I still turn to look for her whenever I smell that scent. Mrs. Evans was alive, exciting, and fun. She was "energy" even while dying with cancer.

In a black and white world, she was color. She was the brilliant pink and yellow and blue and purple and orange of life. She was a redbird, a sunset, a log cabin, a deer running through the woods, or a Bible well worn and marked up with a black Flair. She was a large bowl of popcorn with butter ready to be eaten while sitting by a fireplace on a rainy day. Mrs. Evans was sight, sound, smell, hearing, and touch. She lived a lot of life in one day, and she loved to teach about it. Mrs. Evans loved people—especially those who were needy. She was a giver and a servant.

So for me…the music isn't playing, the candles aren't burning, the candy jars are empty—Mrs. Evans is no longer alive. When I die, I only pray with the Lord's help that I will make one-half the impact on others that she has made on me.

P.S. My dad now has a candy jar, and it's usually always filled.

3

How to Make Children Feel Loved When You Are Busy

Though I am not fond of mothers working full-time while they have children living at home, sometimes it may be necessary. I often think it is a good idea for a mother to work part-time, even if she does have children living at home. The more a mother works, the more vital are her techniques in child rearing and the methods she uses to take advantage of every moment she has with her child. The following two chapters will give several ideas about how to utilize these moments.

1. **Read books and listen to tapes on child rearing.** During the 27 years that I have been married, I have almost always been in the middle of a book on marriage or child rearing.

2. **Do not place too much emphasis on the things that make you busy.** My father was a busy pastor. He traveled and spoke at pastors' conferences for a couple of days out of almost every week. He stayed in nice motels, preached with famous men, and ate delicious meals. But he told me very little about this. I just know because of my own traveling experience. As a child, when I asked my father how his trip went, he would usually reply, "It went fine, but I missed you very much."

I learned from my father. I remember one instance when Jaclynn was a child. She asked, "How did teaching go?" and "Do you like teaching?" to which I replied, "I like teaching, but not as much as I like being your mother."

3.   **Have principles about being away from the family and stick with them.** When my children were small, I began traveling and speaking at ladies' conferences. I made a principle that I would only take an average of one meeting a month in the fall and spring. In the summer and winter, I didn't travel. I quit traveling when my children were teens and started again when our youngest went to college. I still follow my same plan for traveling, even though both of my children are married. Why? Because I have a husband at home and children and grandchildren nearby. I never leave my husband for more than a few days. I think it is unwise for a wife to leave her husband for two or three weeks at a time.

4.   **Let your family know you are available if they need you.** My dad always stressed how his receptionist was to let me straight through should I call on the phone. My husband and I always accept calls at work from our children. The availability of cell phones has helped with this also. I have caller ID, and I always pick up the phone when our children call.

5.   **Make getting up and going to bed especially enjoyable.** My husband did much of his teaching the Bible and reading of Bible stories at bedtime. Why? The children loved to listen because they loved to stay up later. I always sang the same lullaby (to the tune of the traditional children's lullaby) to our children at every nap time and nighttime:

> "Lullaby and good night
> Go to sleep little Jaclynn (Kenny)
> Mommy loves you.
> Daddy loves you.
> And we'll love you all life through.
> Sweet dreams, precious child.
> All the night (nap) God will be with you."

Now Jaclynn sings this same lullaby to her children.

6.   **If you have to, allow your children to stay up an hour later so that you can see your teenage children rather than having them**

go to bed earlier. This was wise advice I received from my father at a time when our children were extremely busy. We made our children's health important, but we didn't put it before our relationship with them.

7.   **Have family slogans.** Ours was "Us four and no more!" At this time our slogan has changed to, "Now we're eight, and this is great!"

8.   **Give each child a separate identity.** My father gave me the following identities when I was just a child:

- "You are a deep thinker."
- "I love it that you think deeply and write your thoughts down on paper." (It is no wonder I am an author and my father's biographer.)
- "You love deeply."

I have always had a fairly good self-esteem even though I have two beautiful older sisters who are very talented.

As a child, I remember seeing the queen of the Tournament of Roses parade while I watched it with my father. "She is beautiful," I commented to my father.

"You are prettier than she is," he replied.

I do not remember becoming conceited about this comment. I remember thinking three things: "Dad really likes me," and "My dad is wonderful!" and "Dad exaggerates to make me feel good."

I still adore him for it.

9.   **Make a praise box for your children.** Cover a small box with wrapping paper. On pretty stationery write 31 things you specifically like about your children. Have your child read one thing a day for a month. Our children and I did this for both sets of their grandparents. I remember that my mom read one thing a day for a month, and my dad read them all the first day!

How to Help Your Children When Their Dad Is Busy

All of these are ideas that I tried with our children when their dad was busy.

1.   Make a praise box for Dad.

- 64 -

2. Have children bring breakfast in bed to Dad.
3. Have children greet Dad when he arrives home or when he leaves for work with his favorite candy, snack, or drink.
4. Bring a picnic supper to Dad at work.
5. Talk often about how much Dad loves them and about what a wonderful Daddy he is!
6. Don't complain about Dad's being gone or make him feel like a stranger when he is around.
7. Plan a special activity for yourself and the children when Dad is extra busy.

On the day that we hitched a sled to our 100-pound yellow Labrador retriever and went sledding down our street, the children and I laughed so hard, it was hard to be miserable that Dad was gone. We had a lot of fun telling him about it when he called.

When you do things for people, you can feel very close to them without spending much time with them. It is important for a mother to solve the problem of her husband's busyness by leading her children to do things for Dad. The mother should be a bridge to keep her children close to their father.

4

LOVING AND RESPECTING YOUR CHILDREN AS A WORKING MOTHER

1. Only work if your husband is 100 percent for it.

2. Make a study of your children's favorite things.

3. Try to give one thing daily, or at least weekly, from the "favorite things" list. Vary the times and ways you give the favorites.

4. Do an unexpected chore or favor for your child weekly.

5. Stop to thank your child for something he has done for you lately.

6. Make a list of good qualities your child possesses that you have not shared with him.

7. Ask your children for their advice.

8. Bring your children with you to a special event.

9. Eat meals as a family and make this time enjoyable.

10. Drive places together. Driving time is good talking time. I enjoyed being my children's taxicab driver (most of the time).

11. Call your child by pet names.

12. Have a daily or weekly time alone with each child doing something that each enjoys.

13. Have a family night and serve the same thing (i.e. homemade pizza) each night.

14. Have a childlike, playful spirit.

15. Do all of your work at work, if possible.

16. Give your child a separate identity. Tell him why you need him. Make him feel exclusive.

17. Work together.

18. Exercise together.

19. Go soul winning and do things for others together.

20. Do special things for Dad together.

21. Bake a pie for the youth director or for the principal together.

22. Sing together.

23. Pray together.

24. Fast together about a special need or decision.

25. Wait up for dates and activities and talk about them.

26. Share jokes and cartoons with them.

27. Leave notes and cards in unexpected places.

28. Share their sports interests and so forth. Attend their special events.

29. Smile at them in a crowd.

30. Get on their eye level and say "hello" each time you see them. Then hug them tightly.

5

WHAT TO DO WHEN OVERWHELMED

The following are some tips and helps on honoring and exalting your husband while being overwhelmed with rearing young children.

1.   Ask your husband if you can have a weekly scheduled date time. This is one of my two first suggestions for having a happy marriage. My husband and I have practiced this since the beginning of our marriage and continue to do so today. All couples have time for this, as much as they have time to schedule eating or sleeping.

We find time to do what we want to do. Have a date time, even if it means going to the corner coffee shop for a cup of coffee and coming home an hour later. My husband and I did this for a while in our poorer days.

2.   Put your children on a schedule. I highly recommend reading and applying the the principles in the book *My First 300 Babies* by Gladys West Hendrick (Hurst Publishing, Goleta, California, 1964). I used this book almost as much as my Bible in rearing our children when they were infants and preschoolers. Mrs. Hendrick includes schedules to follow in the rearing of children. This book can be obtained from the Hyles-Anderson College Bookstore, 8400 Burr Street, Crown Point, Indiana 46307. I strongly believe this book belongs in every mother's personal library.

3.   Put your children in bed early. When our children were little, we put them in bed by 8:00 p.m. (other than church nights).

4. **Teach your children while they are very young to play alone in their rooms for a small amount of time each day.**

5. **Do special projects for your husband with your children.** This will make you and your children feel close to your husband when you may not see him often. A candy bar card would be a good example.

6. **Teach your children to run after their daddy.** Bring him supper at the office. Teach them to build their schedule around their daddy's and not to expect him to build his schedule around theirs.

7. **Use your imagination.** Ideas beget ideas, and excuses beget excuses. I had to push the reset button often.

I practiced all of these at some time(s) when our children were little. They are now adults, and I don't regret doing any of them.

Part III-Training Children

*To be good is noble, but to teach others
how to be good is nobler—and less trouble.*
–Mark Twain

1

TRAINING THROUGH SONG

Now that we have covered the first two steps of discipline, prayer and love, I would like to discuss the next step, which is teaching. One of the main reasons God gives us children is to teach or to train them. Unfortunately, most parents busy themselves with their jobs and careers, paying for their four-bedroom homes, and they have time to do everything **but** train their children.

When our children were small, I trained them mostly through song. I thought of the most important subjects that I wanted them to learn, and I began to sing to them about those subjects. For example, I wanted our children to learn to be saved as soon as they could understand. One of the first songs I sang to them was:

> "Thank You, Lord, for saving my soul.
> Thank You, Lord, for making me whole.
> Thank You, Lord, for giving to me
> Thy great salvation so rich and free."

I wanted them to learn about the Bible. I sang:

> "The B-I-B-L-E
> Yes, that's the Book for me.
> I stand alone on the Word of God.
> The B-I-B-L-E."

I wanted them to learn good self-esteem. I sang:

"God made you special.
You're the only one of your kind.
God gave you a body
And a bright, healthy mind.
He had a special purpose
He wanted you to find.
That's why He made you very special.
You're the only one of your kind."

I wanted our son to learn to be masculine. I sang with boldness:

"Dare to be a Daniel.
Dare to stand alone.
Dare to have a purpose firm.
Dare to make it known."

As our children became preschoolers, books were added to songs as their curriculum. I chose books that taught shapes, colors, numbers, and Christian values. At a scheduled time each day, we moved to our next training ground which was a couch. We cuddled up beside each other, and I read them many fun books, as well as educational ones.

I remember going to Toys R Us when our children were three and four year olds and finding as many workbooks for their age as I could. These workbooks taught phonics and concepts like simple math. We began to spend some of our time together playing school. Jaclynn and Kenny had to raise their hand before they were called upon. I was so excited to play school that our children became excited too. School also consisted of playtime and treat time so that it was never a boring experience. Both of our children went to school knowing how to read small words, as well as having many months of behavioral practice. Neither of them was bored in kindergarten, however, and they excelled.

I did not tell my friends about our children's accomplishments, though I do remember vividly calling my husband at work to tell him that Jaclynn had just read her first word. I felt so privileged that I got to be with her instead of a teacher when she read her first word.

I never trained our children so that I could prove they were smarter than someone else's child. I did not train them to pressure them. I simply did what is one of the keys to rearing good children: I enjoyed them. I felt that spending time with and enjoying Jaclynn and Kenny was a great gift from God that would only last a short time.

I had noticed that most older women I know said the same thing, "Enjoy them while you can; they grow up so fast," while most of the younger women seemed harried and irritated about the children God had given them to enjoy. I decided that I would enjoy my children while I had them and then enjoy the empty nest when they were grown.

I couldn't think of **enough** ways to train our children. When Jaclynn was small, I bought her a tiny keyboard and then a larger one. I taught her all I knew about the piano. I was afraid I was doing her future piano teacher more harm than good, but Jaclynn learned swiftly at the piano. She is now one of our three church pianists, as well as teaching private piano lessons in her home. I feel that Jaclynn was relaxed with the piano before she took her first "real" lesson. She became familiar with the piano in her own bedroom with her own mother having fun with her by playing the keyboard.

I have never become a good seamstress, but when Jaclynn was about eight years old, I began to sew with her every weekend. As it turned out, she did not excel at sewing. That did not bother me. My purpose was not to push her. I simply wished to provide as many opportunities as I could for her. More than that, I wanted to enjoy life with her.

Though I am a lousy athlete, I taught our children as many sports as I could, as did their dad. In some sporting activities, I taught them to tease Mom more than anything; I was horrible. In all sporting activities, we had a lot of fun!

As much as I enjoyed teaching our children, my husband and I chose not to homeschool them. Our church has a wonderful Christian school system. For all of the years that our children attended Hammond Baptist Schools, I had almost no complaints. What complaints I had were kept to myself. The supporting of other authorities is another vital child-rearing tactic, which will be discussed further in another chapter. Because most of our children's friends were at our church and those children would all be going to school, my husband and I thought it best to send our children to school. We did not want to cause our children to be ostracized unnecessarily. We would have gladly had them be ostracized rather than to put them in a public school. But we are very grateful that we had the chance to put them in the church schools that were opened when my father was the pastor. I am thankful for my father's vision and for the sacrifices of the many church members who helped to start Hammond Baptist Schools. I attended the same Hammond Baptist Schools that our children did. The teachers at Hammond Baptist Schools are the best, and they were very good to both Jaclynn and Kenny.

As our children began elementary school, I saw homework as an opportunity. It was a time each day when I could bond with our children and also share with their teachers in their training process.

Jaclynn and Kenny came home from school to a snack and a fun time with Mom. But at a scheduled time each day (usually right after supper), they were required to do their homework, and I always was by their side to help them. When there was a history fair or a science fair, I did not do these projects for our children, but I was very involved in helping them. I helped with cheerleading projects and sports projects. Other than homework and small daily chores such as cleaning their rooms and making their beds, most of my other training during the school-age years took place during the summer.

Several summers I had our children clean house with me. Our house has eight rooms. I wrote down what needed to be done in each room, and then I assigned three rooms for Jaclynn to clean and three for Kenny to clean. I cleaned the other two. When you work with someone, you get to know them well. Our family worked together a lot, and we became very close. Each week I changed the rooms that they cleaned so they would have some knowledge of how to clean any room.

I appreciate my husband for many things. One is for being an excellent father. Each time he had a chore to do around the house, he involved our son in the task. He started this training when Kenny was barely big enough to hold a hammer. Kenny learned many skills through this, but most of all he learned to be masculine and to be close to his dad.

When Kenny was 12 years old, I stopped having him do feminine chores around the house. Our family had a tractor at the time, which we used to mow our acre yard. We sold our tractor and bought a push mower. Kenny then became in charge of mowing the lawn and all yard work. For several years, our family had an above ground pool. Jaclynn and Kenny did all of the maintenance of the pool. Their dad taught them; I never even learned how to care for it.

One summer I gave my daughter a certain amount of cash from our grocery budget, and I drove her to the grocery store and dropped her off once a week. Jaclynn had to make a menu list and a grocery list beforehand. Then she had to buy groceries with the allotted amount of cash. She did all of the grocery shopping for the whole summer. The first time Jaclynn went, she seemed overly confident. She seemed to have the common philosophy that it seems most teenagers have: how hard could Mom's work be anyway? When she returned to the car, she was flustered. She had had to put some groceries back because she had gone over budget. This was exactly the kind of lesson I wanted her to learn.

One summer Jaclynn did all of the laundry for the whole family. One summer she prepared dinner for the family once a week. Jaclynn and I baked together frequently. I thought of as many ideas as I could to train our children. When I worked, they worked, and most of the time, when they worked, I worked. When it came time to plant flowers, we all planted hundreds of them. For several years we had a vegetable garden that we all did together. I knew nothing about vegetable gardening, but I saw gardening as a wonderful opportunity to train and to get to know my children. The children were required to help plant, weed, water, and harvest. Many summers we went to U-pick farms and picked fruits and vegetables together. I did with our children during their teen years what I had done in their childhood: I enjoyed them, knowing that my time to train them was passing more and more quickly.

2

TRAINING THROUGH
FAMILY DEVOTIONS

Our parents trained my brother, my sisters, and me by having family devotions during our childhood years. During our family altar, as we called it, we memorized several Psalms and other verses. Dad also acted out Bible stories and taught us character lessons. We practiced such things as answering the phone properly, answering the door properly and so forth. We prayed together at the end of every family altar. Dad, David, and I prayed every other night, and Mom, Becky and Linda prayed every other night.

When we became teenagers, our schedules became busier, and our family altar ceased. Our training did not, however. Though both parents trained us, my fondest memories are of times spent around the kitchen table late at night. Dad would sit with us and philosophize with us about life. He loved to teach about marriage and child rearing. He also used our current situations with our school and our peers to train us. Sometimes Dad would spontaneously decide to teach us something in the kitchen, like how to make a Texas-style hamburger or how to make an omelet, which were two of his specialties. Whatever Dad taught, he taught it with enthusiasm. Dad loved life, and he loved to teach. Therefore, everything he taught became fun to us. I often went to my parents for advice around the kitchen table or as we were riding in the car. I also received much training from them in this way.

I was engaged to be married for 12 months. During those months, my dad met with me once a week to talk about marriage. He especially wanted to teach me about the intimate marital relationship from a man's perspective. He was always completely proper in his approach, but he was honest and truthful. I have often recalled the lessons learned during this year of my life. They have been invaluable to my marriage.

When Jaclynn was engaged, I tried to teach her the lessons that my dad had taught me about marriage. My husband did the same thing with our son and our son-in-law. I was always very open with our children, even when they came to me with the most personal of questions. I gave them as much information as I thought was appropriate for them to handle at that age. I strived to never act shocked about their questions, and I thanked them for coming to me with them.

Kenny once asked me why children with good Christian parents turn out wrong. I told him it was because they quit telling their mom and dad everything, and I meant it. Good communication is vital to child rearing and part of proper training.

In closing to this section of teaching, I would like to give you a few points:

1. **It is the father's responsibility to teach the Bible to the children.** I can be a very pious woman, sometimes in a good way and sometimes in a not-so-good way. There came a time in my life when I felt that my Bible training of our children was doing more harm than good. From that time on, even though I was with our children more than their dad was, I left the Bible training to him. I did not want the children to see me taking the spiritual leadership of the home. I felt that I could best teach the Bible to Jaclynn and Kenny by teaching them to honor God through their father, and I do not regret the approach that I chose. One of the greatest hindrances to good child rearing is an overly pious mother who does not fulfill her proper role in the home. Even if a father fails to train his children, submission on the part of the mother is one of the most vital lessons a mother can learn and teach.

2. **A mother should teach her children how to work.** Though I believe it is important that a father take part in this aspect of training, it is the mother who spends the most time with her children. By teaching them how to work and working with them, the mother helps her

children to know her better. If a mother lives a Christian life that is the "pattern of good works" that Titus 2:7 talks about, she can train her children about the Bible through her life. *"In all things shewing thyself a pattern of good works: in doctrine showing uncorruptness, gravity, sincerity."*

3. Make teaching spontaneous and fun. When Jaclynn and Kenny were small, I had a more rigid and scheduled approach to training them. Though I still am a fan of schedule, my approach to training changed. I noticed that my husband chose to train spontaneously while our family was having a fun time together. We would be taking a walk, and he would point out something in nature and begin to talk about God. Jaclynn and Kenny would seem to hang on every word he spoke, while they often seemed bored and barely awake when I taught them.

One evening I looked out one of our back windows and saw my husband and our two children lying on our deck. My rigid personality said to myself, "What will our neighbors think?" After watching them have fun without me for several minutes, I changed my thinking: "If you can't beat them, join them." I laid down on the deck and heard Jaclynn and Kenny ask their dad several deep questions about the sky, the moon, and the stars. Pretty soon, a fascinating talk about God developed. Our children learned a lot about God that night, and I learned a lot about training children.

PART IV-SCHEDULING CHILDREN

A schedule is your friend.
–Dr. Jack Hyles

1

SCHEDULING AS A MEANS TO SUCCESS

The fifth step to rearing a disciplined child is scheduling. For 23 years I have worked with college students as a teacher at Hyles-Anderson College. I have worked with many young ladies who sincerely wanted to do right. They wanted to complete their projects and make good grades in class, but they failed. Why? Many times it is because no one has taught them how to organize their time. Good Christian people with sincere hearts sometimes fail repeatedly in their Christian lives and then become defeated because they were not taught as children how to organize their time to accomplish the things they need to accomplish in order to achieve success.

REASONS TO SCHEDULE OUR CHILDREN

1. **When children are scheduled from infancy, the marriage of the parents does not have to suffer.** The parents can still have time alone, and they can predict when that time will be.

2. **When children are scheduled from infancy, the parents are afforded the privilege of getting to know each child individually.** One child plays alone while another child receives individual attention, etc. This is especially beneficial to the child who is a follower or to the child who is shy.

3. **Scheduling allows us to give attention to our children when they are acting positively.** The parent who does not have scheduled time for his children will give them attention mainly when they are misbehaving. Therefore, lack of schedule promotes poor behavior. The scheduled child learns that if he behaves, he will have some special time with mother soon.

4. **Scheduled children learn to be balanced children.** They learn how to be good at many different things. They learn how to put aside one task when it is time to complete another. They learn not only to work hard, but they learn **how** to organize themselves so that they **can** work hard.

5. **Scheduling relieves guilt on the part of the parents.** When mothers are extra busy, they struggle mostly with feeling guilty about neglecting their children. When children have scheduled time with Mom or Dad, Mom does not need to feel guilty when she is busy working.

6. **Scheduling prevents overly-dependent children.** For example, though I scheduled time to rock my children, I did not rock them to sleep unless they were ill. Because of this, my children went to sleep quickly and did not have to sleep in Mom and Dad's room, etc.

7. **Scheduling prevents boredom.** A child's schedule should include many different changes of scenery and activity so he will not become bored. Boredom is one of the most common causes of misbehavior in children.

8. **Scheduling teaches an enjoyment for being alone and alleviates fear.** This will draw a child toward God. My children had a scheduled time each day, even as babies, when they were required to play alone in their rooms. (Safety precautions should be taken, of course.) This teaches a child how to entertain himself.

9. **Scheduling prevents the parent from leaning too much on the television for baby-sitting.**

A Basic Schedule for Children of All Ages

Of course, this schedule may need to be adjusted for your household. The following schedules worked well for us.

A Schedule for Newborn Babies
(Begin at Two Weeks Old)

2:00 a.m.	Nurse or feed baby
	(This can be eliminated at 2-3 months.)
6:00 a.m.	Nurse or feed baby
9:00 a.m.	Nurse or feed baby
9:30 a.m.	Sing time
10:00 a.m.	Play time (Baby occupies self)
10:30 a.m.	Bathe and dress baby
11:00 a.m.	Nurse baby
11:30 a.m.	Nap
2:30 p.m.	Nurse or feed baby
3:00 p.m.	Sing time
3:30 p.m.	Wake time (Baby should spend **some** time occupying himself.)
5:00 p.m.	Lotion rub
5:30 p.m.	Nurse or feed baby
6:00 p.m.	Bedtime
10:00 p.m.	Nurse or feed baby

A Schedule for Older Babies
(Begin at 6-9 Months Old.)

7:00 a.m.	Nurse or bottle
7:30 a.m.	Breakfast
8:00 a.m.	Bath and dress
8:30 a.m.	Play in room or in playpen
9:30 a.m.	Nap
10:30 a.m.	Play in walker in living room
12:00 noon	Lunch

12:30 p.m.	Time with Mom
1:00 p.m.	Nap
2:30 p.m.	Playtime
5:00 p.m.	Swing or jumpseat
5:30 p.m.	Supper
6:00 p.m.	Bedtime

A Schedule for Preschool Children

7:30 a.m.	Breakfast
8:00 a.m.	Dress
8:30 a.m.	Clean room
9:00 a.m.	Play time
10:00 a.m.	Snack time
10:30 a.m.	Help Mommy
11:00 a.m.	Play time (in another chosen location)
12:00 noon	Lunch
12:30 p.m.	Time with Mom
	(Teach basic school skills, Bible stories, songs, etc.)
1:00 p.m.	Nap time
2:30 p.m.	Play with Mommy
	(Do something fun the child enjoys.)
4:30 p.m.	Help Mom
5:00 p.m.	Dinner
6:00 p.m.	Time with family
7:00 p.m.	Bathe and get ready for bed
8:00 p.m.	Pray, sing, and go to bed

A Schedule for Grade School Children

6:30 a.m.	Get up, dress, straighten room, read Bible, and pray
7:00 a.m.	Breakfast
7:15 a.m.	Brush teeth, comb hair, and clean ears
7:30 a.m.	Chores for Mom (especially if she works outside the home)
8:15 a.m.	School (Time for mom to do household work chores or personal work)

3:15 p.m.	Picked up from school
4:00 p.m.	After school snack and talk with Mom
4:30 p.m.	Play time, unwind
5:30 p.m.	Practice lesson (Set a time for piano, etc., and do not allow them to go over.)
6:00 p.m.	Dinner
7:00 p.m.	Play with Mom / Homework
8:00 p.m.	Time to relax near the family
8:45 p.m.	Get ready for bed (Bathe, set out clothes, and shine shoes.)
9:00 p.m.	Bedtime (Pray and sing with them. Allow 15 minutes to listen to a tape or read in bed.)
9:15 p.m.	Lights out

A Schedule for Teenagers

6:00 a.m.	Get up and have devotions
6:30 a.m.	Dress, clean room
7:00 a.m.	Breakfast
7:15 a.m.	Fix hair, brush teeth, etc.
7:30 a.m.	Do chores for Mom
7:40 a.m.	Leave for school (Pray in the car.)
8:00 a.m.	School
3:15 p.m.	Teenagers' activities

Teens' activities and arrival home will vary. Have them list, in order, what they need to do daily, and approve it. Encourage them to do their work first, but allow them to intersperse some fun. Check the list to find a time that you can spend with them, even if it is just hanging around and talking and asking their opinions for a while. Schedule this time as early as possible in the evening so you are not feeling "draggy," especially if you are a morning person.

A SCHEDULE FOR ADULT CHILDREN

Each week schedule time to write to them and tell them something you like about them. Remember to call and ask for their advice and opinions from time to time, especially in their individual areas of expertise. Die to self and try to be there when they need you, while allowing both yourself and your children to build your own lives. Pray for them.

My husband and I have a scheduled family night every two weeks with our adult children and grandchildren. Every other Tuesday evening we meet, usually for dinner and playing games. We also have our children over every Sunday for dinner. Once every two weeks I also have a lunch or shopping date with the girls—our daughter, granddaughter, and daughter-in-law. At the time of this writing, our date is scheduled to take place on Friday afternoons.

Scheduling time with adult children keeps the relationship close and also keeps the parents from interrupting at times that would be inconvenient for their married children. Even though Todd and Jaclynn live just a mile away from us, I almost never drop in without calling. I am rarely at our daughter's house when our son-in-law is home, and I rarely call when Todd is home.

I also have a scheduled time to baby-sit our granddaughter on Saturday mornings. Some weeks I may see my family many other times rather than during the scheduled times, but having a scheduled time together keeps our relationships close during those many extra busy times of our lives. For long-distance relationships, a weekly scheduled telephone time, e-mail time, or letter time would be helpful.

PART V–PUNISHING CHILDREN

If punishment makes not the will supple,
it hardens the offender.
–Locke

1

PUNISHMENT

Though punishment is just **part** of discipline and last in importance on my list, punishment **is** important, and it must be carried out properly to rear a good child.

There is little need for punishment until a child begins to crawl. At six to nine months, when a baby begins to crawl, he will need to have his hand spanked from time to time in order to keep from hurting himself. A child about to put his finger into an electrical outlet needs to learn to understand what the word "no" means.

I was not one of those mothers who filled my home with breakable and expensive knickknacks. Neither was I the kind of mother who put away all of my delicate pretties until our children were older. It is wise for a mother to find a compromise in this area and to teach her baby what he may or may not touch. Spanking the hand is the tool which teaches a baby what the word "no" means. Other than the firm, but brief swat of the hand, there is no need for the new parent to do anything but love, care for, and pray for his child.

When our children began to walk, we began to spank them periodically. It is my experience that if a child is spanked wisely, there will be little need to spank him past the age of 12. Also, when proper spanking is done, those spankings are infrequent and become less and less frequent until the child is too old for them. I believe that most of the time, spanking done during the teenage years causes rebellion. I have seen some teenage boys, however, who I thought needed a "spanking 'til it hurt" from their father. A teenage boy who has not had his will molded properly might need a spanking, but rarely does spanking work in the teenage years; neither should it be necessary.

When our children were small, my husband and I listed seven reasons why we would spank our children. They were:

1. Direct disobedience
2. Disrespectful talk to authority (sassing)
3. Physical fighting
4. Lying/Cheating
5. Stealing
6. Getting in trouble at school
7. Throwing a temper tantrum

We did not necessarily need to use all of these, but they were the seven reasons we spanked them. We did **not** spank our children for the following reasons.

1. **Clumsiness.** They were not spanked for spilling their milk.
2. **Inconvenience.** They were not spanked because they inconvenienced their parents.
3. **Ignorance.** If I did not think a rule was clear, I did not spank our children until they had been given one fair warning. After one warning, however, we did spank them. Two or more warnings would have been only meaningless threats.

PROCEDURE

The following is the procedure I used to spank our children for breaking any of the seven rules.

1. Place the child in a room by himself. I recommend the bathroom because there are no toys or distractions.

2. Go alone to pray. Ask the Lord to give you wisdom to properly love and punish the child. Ask the Lord to help the child to learn what he needs to learn from the spanking.

3. Go to the child and repeat several times the rule which has been broken. For example, "You told a lie," and the rule is, "When you tell a lie, you get a spanking."

4.   Assure your child of his worth and your love. You might say, "I love you, and I don't want to spank you, but the rule says that I have to. You are not bad, but throwing a fit is bad."

5.   Spank your child slowly, one blow at a time. Usually five swats are sufficient, but spank until the child cries. Using a paddle is not my first choice but may be necessary if a parent is not strong enough to hurt the child. Tears will let you know if your spanking is hurting him enough to teach him.

6.   Leave the child and go to pray, again asking the Lord to give you wisdom and to help the child to understand.

7.   Return to the child and pray with him, allowing the child to hear you asking God to teach him that "telling a lie is bad, but Jaclynn is not bad." Allow him to hear you asking God to help him to know that you love him.

8.   Have the child pray.

9.   Express affection to the child. If the child has been spanked properly, he will be the first to initiate the affection. Wait to give him a chance to do this. If he does not, go ahead and hug him, but take note. Something should be changed before the next spanking. The spanking was not done properly.

This is the method of spanking I recommend for an infraction of any of the previously mentioned rules listed on page 89.

2

PUNISHMENT AND THE STRONG-WILLED CHILD

When our daughter Jaclynn was two and one-half, she began to throw temper tantrums. She had been almost a perfect child from birth until this point. Suddenly she began to lie on the floor and kick and scream for long periods of time. Once or twice she did this until she vomited. The slightest thing could set her off, and this became a regular occurrence.

I sought counsel from both my pastor/father and from my husband and formulated the following plan:

1. I ignored her tantrums until she stopped crying. I simply continued to go about my business.

2. I tried to act confident. Children misbehave more when they feel their parents are rattled, angry, or frustrated.

3. When the crying ceased, I put Jaclynn in a "timeout" place. I chose a place where there were no toys. Our "timeout" place was the bathroom.

4. I told Jaclynn that she was going to be spanked and that she was to let me know when she was ready.

5. I checked with Jaclynn periodically to see if she was ready to bend herself over my knee for a spanking.

6. If she said "no," I continued about my business once more and left her in the "timeout" place. I continued to check if she was ready every five minutes or so.

7.   When she said "yes," I explained to her the wrongdoing and the following rule, **"When you throw a fit, you get a spanking."**

8.   I asked Jaclynn to bend over my knee and proceeded with a spanking and followed the steps outlined in the previous chapter.

Before I began using this plan, I had been spanking Jaclynn for her tantrums but seemed to be getting nowhere in breaking her will. I was having to force Jaclynn over my knee. Because Jaclynn was very strong for her age and unwilling to be spanked, it seemed a semi-wrestling match was taking place. I was unwilling for this behavior to continue. Remember, I do not believe in child abuse; I only believe in Biblical chastening, which is a calm spanking on the child's posterior.

My husband suggested that I wait until Jaclynn was ready to bend over my knee herself. The first time I tried this method, I just knew that Jaclynn was going to be in the "timeout" place until she was 18. As I recall, it took about 15 minutes before Jaclynn was willing to be spanked. The second or third time I tried this, it only took about five minutes. This was the beginning of the end of Jaclynn's "terrible twos" stage, and since that time until this writing, Jaclynn has given nothing but delight to my husband and me. We rarely had to punish her during her grade school years. Jaclynn received her last spanking when she was about 10, and she was a joy to have in our home all during her teen years and until she married at age 21. Today she is one of the sweetest Christians I know. She and I are the best of friends.

THE STRONG-WILLED TEENAGER

I would like to begin this section by saying how proud I am of our son Ken. He graduated from Hyles-Anderson College and has completed his first year of teaching at Hammond Baptist Junior High School. At this writing, he is working for Brother Schaap and is a great help to him. On December 17, 2005, he married a wonderful girl, Candace Hooker. Ken and Candace are exactly the kind of son and daughter-in-law I dreamed of and prayed for. However, when our son was a very young teenager, we found some pretty rough music in his school bag. This was music that Kenny knew he was forbidden to listen to as long as he lived in our house.

I prayed daily that if our children did wrong, God would help them to get caught. I believe it was God Who helped me to "accidentally" find the music. I also believe it was of the Lord that my husband was home at the time. He just happened to have taken a rare day off of work.

We handled Kenny's time of rebellion in the following ways.

1. **We punished him.**
   A. Kenny received a spanking from his father. Though I believe it is not usually profitable or necessary to spank a child after the age of 12, in Kenny's case, I think it was the best thing.
   B. Kenny had to smash both his tapes and his walkman. Kenny's tapes belonged to someone else; he was merely borrowing them. Therefore, Kenny had to inform his friend at school that he could not return his music to him.
   C. Kenny lost television privileges and dating privileges for 30 days.

Before this episode, I taught that a child should not be punished in more than one way for one offense. I still believe that to usually be the case. As I look back, however, I believe with all of my heart that my husband handled Kenny's infraction properly. The type of music Kenny was listening to was much more serious than a two year old's tantrum. Kenny got the message loud and clear that his father would not tolerate this type of music in our home. Some of the other teenagers at Kenny's school told Kenny that their parents knew they listened to this music but would not do anything about it. Kenny learned that day that he had a masculine father who would do something about it. A few hours after Kenny received his punishment, he hugged my husband and said, "Dad, you are the best friend I have." They are still the best of friends.

2. **We spent more time with him.** I believe one of the reasons for Kenny's rebellion was my fault. It was Jaclynn's senior year of high school, and I had determined to be involved in making it a great year for her. Jaclynn and I did a lot of things together, things that Kenny was not interested in doing. I had not neglected Kenny fully but had left him at home alone too much.

After this event, I began to take Kenny with Jaclynn and me most of the time. If we were going shopping, Kenny went along. Kenny would sometimes say, "Shopping is no fun."

I replied, "We will make it fun," and we tried our best to do so. I incorporated things into Jaclynn's and my activities that Kenny would enjoy. I learned that it is unwise to leave a teenager home alone much of the time. I had a long talk with Kenny and told him it was not our job to trust him; it was his parents' job to protect him.

3. We came together as a team and had every family member do his part. I also had a long talk with Jaclynn. I told her that a family is a team, and when one team member is in trouble, all the other team members must join together to help that person. I exhorted our daughter to make it her personal challenge to help our son. Jaclynn proved herself to be a help as she began to do her part to help her brother.

One thing Jaclynn did was begin to sing with Kenny. Jaclynn would play Christian songs on the piano, and Kenny would sing along with her. Sometimes I would join in. The song I remember most still brings tears to my eyes when I think of it. All of our family joined together to replace Kenny's wrong music with the right kind of music. This theory of replacement is important in dealing with problems with teenagers.

Kenny proved himself to be a tender-hearted Christian. He became closer to his father than ever, and Kenny went on to grow in the Lord and make us proud of him.

I believe that my husband and I, through the grace of God, were successful in breaking the wills of our children, one at age two and the other as a young teenager. We broke their wills, but we did not break their spirits. Both of our children have remained our dearest friends into their adult years, and yet they married, left the nest and have built successful lives apart from us. Both are serving the Lord full-time and are faithful to the church their father pastors, the church they have attended since babyhood.

Our children and their parents are not perfect. Though I believe in both of our children, only time will tell whether or not their spirits will stay tender toward the Lord. But looking back, I have no regrets on how my husband and I handled their strong-willed times.

3

More Helps on Correction

Please allow me to share some additional tips and helps on the subject of punishment that would be helpful to use in the rearing of children.

1. Use positive methods. One of the most common questions I am asked regarding child rearing is this: "What should a mother do when her child is misbehaving in public?" Every parent has had a whining, crying child in the cart at the grocery store and has wondered what to do. First of all, let me say that I do not believe a child should EVER be spanked in a public place. A public place would be anywhere except for a house, preferably your own. I would not spank a child in a car, in a store restroom, or in any public place. As soon as a child is old enough to remember why he is being spanked when he gets home, the parent should spank a child who misbehaves publicly. Until that time, however, being in public with a small child can be difficult.

I recommend trying a positive method for a small child who has a short memory span. Before the child has a chance to misbehave, offer that child a treat for good behavior. Much extra planning needs to go into taking a young toddler on a shopping spree. Thought should be given ahead of time on how to make this as pleasant an experience as possible for the child and for everyone involved. It is not proper to threaten or scold your child in the grocery store; those around should not have to listen to it.

When our daughter was in her "terrible twos" stage, I did not regularly take her out to restaurants and other places until this phase of her life had passed. She did go to church, but other than that, she was home most of the time. A mother who is struggling with a lot of public misbehavior by her toddler may be keeping her child away from home too much of the time. It takes a lot of time at home to properly train a child, and part of that training is spanking. A mother with a misbehaving child also may be failing to plan ahead and to use as many positive methods as possible to prevent misbehavior.

When a child is old enough to understand why he is being spanked when he gets home, the wise mother will still use positive methods in pubic situations or in private situations for that matter. Nothing is wrong with telling a child that if he is good in the store, he will receive a small treat. That treat does not always have to be something expensive or laden with sugar. There is nothing wrong with making an otherwise boring experience to be made enjoyable. It is a good idea to make time with Mom an exciting time, rather than a time for a mother to dare her child to disobey her. A child can be offered a treat **before** he misbehaves, but he should never be given a treat **because** he is misbehaving in order to quiet him down. Nor should a child ever be given a treat that he has whined for.

Jaclynn's second grade teacher, Mrs. Doris Smith, asked me to come in to her classroom for a parent/teacher conference. When I came in, she informed me that Jaclynn was repeatedly failing to finish her class work. Mrs. Smith did not feel that Jaclynn was being disobedient or lazy. She said that she watched Jaclynn erasing her letters and writing them over and over until they were perfect. During the time that Jaclynn lived in our home, I frequently saw in her signs of perfectionism, especially in the area of handwork.

Jaclynn had a problem, and her teacher needed us to help her fix it. But Jaclynn's problem didn't fall under any of the categories that we would spank her for. Therefore, we chose to use a positive method. We talked to Jaclynn about perfectionism and told her that we would take her to Dairy Queen if she finished all of her schoolwork for one week. At the end of the week, Mrs. Smith informed us that Jaclynn had finished all of her work. Not only was that particular problem solved, but also we were never called in for another parent/teacher conference. Of course, always follow through with any promises made when using positive discipline.

Spanking is a vital Biblical part of punishment. It **should** be used, but it should be used sparingly. When parents automatically use a lot of positive methods in their discipline, spanking will not need to be used often, especially as the child leaves his baby and toddler years.

2.   **Do not threaten a child.** I am not against giving one fair warning to a child in any case. A second warning becomes a threat, and this is an ineffective tool in child rearing. Always follow through with a spanking once a warning has been given. Making warnings and threats without following through is one of the most common mistakes made by parents. Examples of this can be seen almost everywhere you look in public places.

When a parent has consistent rules for spanking, he will be less likely to make a warning without following through. Be sure you have a valid reason to spank before you open your mouth with a warning. It has been said that consistency is the key to rearing good children. I don't know if there is such a thing as a completely consistent parent, but having predetermined rules for spanking takes a parent several steps closer to the goal of consistency.

3.   **Make the punishment fit the crime.** When our son Kenny was a child, he hated vegetables. Trying to get Kenny to eat cabbage was more frightening than watching a horror movie. We spanked Kenny several times trying to teach him to eat foods that were good for him, but to no avail. Finally, we realized that Kenny's problem was not disobedience or any other problem on our spanking list. I believe he really became physically ill at the taste of cabbage.

We still needed to discipline Kenny in the area of proper eating habits, so we had to find a punishment to fit the crime. Kenny's crime was not rebellion. Instead, it seemed to be a genuine distaste for most things healthy. My husband and I made a new rule. We set a timer, and if Kenny did not eat his required one helping of vegetables at dinner, he was given a second helping. This new rule fixed our dilemma. Kenny never did learn to like vegetables while he lived at our house, but he did learn to eat one helping at every meal without causing an unpleasant time at the table.

4. **Never yell at a child and never hit a child anywhere except on his hand or his bottom.** There is a great problem with physical and verbal abuse in our society today. Because of this, some would say that spanking a child is wrong. The commandment to spank is given very clearly in the Bible. I do not think it is the spanking parent who abuses his child. I believe that child abuse is caused mainly by two things: (1) Parental addictions to things such as drugs, alcohol, and sexual immorality cause most child abuse. I believe a parent with such addictions should confess his need for help and should get into a Biblical-based addiction program as soon as possible. The grace of God and accountability are keys to overcoming addictions. (2) A parent's failure to properly discipline a child causes child abuse. Neither of these are excuses for child abuse; they are reasons. THERE IS NO EXCUSE FOR CHILD ABUSE!

A parent who does not follow the Bible plan for disciplining and punishing a child will have a naughty child. When the parent becomes exasperated with a naughty child and has no plan to follow, that parent will lose control and will yell, curse, and hit the child. Curse words and words such as "shut up" should have no place in child discipline.

5. **Never spank a child immediately.** If a parent sends a child to a particular place for a spanking and then goes alone to pray first, that parent's temper will be controlled by the time he administers punishment.

6. **Don't correct a child publicly.** Many times a parent corrects a child publicly because he has failed to correct a child privately. A child should be treated with respect just as much as an adult should be. It is usually inappropriate to correct another adult publicly, and it is a habit that should not be developed with a child. If our children failed to say "thank you" or to practice good manners in a public place, I made it a habit **not** to correct them. I set aside a time to go over such manners at home.

Sometimes I was embarrassed as I watched other parents correct their child as I failed to correct mine. But I believe my caution to show extra respect to them publicly and to train them privately gave my children and myself better manners in the long run.

PUNISHING TEENAGERS

As stated earlier, spanking rarely is effective in punishing a teenager, and a properly punished child should not have to be punished much as a teenager. The withholding of privileges such as using the car or attending social activities is the most effective tool in punishing teenagers. Never punish by not allowing your child to attend church or a church activity. This will squelch the spiritual effect that the church can have on your child. Also, never punish your child by making him work. This will make work distasteful to the child. I have two other bits of advice for the parents of teenagers.

    1. **Don't embarrass your teenager.** There is never a time to show disrespect to any age child. I went to high school with two boys whose father would shave their heads as a punishment. Shaving the head was not popular in the 1970s when I was in high school. Only the "nerds" had shaved heads. This form of punishment was humiliating to these boys. They were mocked and teased at school. Even as a teenager, I remember thinking that these boys whose parents were workers in our church were going to be turned off by church because of their father's behavior. Both of these boys have struggled much in their adult life.

    2. **Don't prolong the punishment.** I believe as a general rule it is better for a parent to give a stricter punishment that lasts a week or two than prolonging any punishment for a month. A child should not continue to suffer for an infraction that was committed weeks or months before. Neither should a child's mistakes be brought up in the future once they have been dealt with.

BIBLICAL INSTRUCTION REGARDING PUNISHMENT

Proverbs 13:24   *"He that spareth his rod hateth his son: but he that loveth him chasteneth him betimes."*

Proverbs 19:18	*"Chasten thy son while there is hope, and let not thy soul spare for his crying."*
Proverbs 22:15	*"Foolishness is bound in the heart of a child; but the rod of correction shall drive it far from him."*
Proverbs 23:13, 14	*"Withhold not correction from the child: for if thou beatest him with the rod, he shall not die. Thou shalt beat him with the rod, and shalt deliver his soul from hell.*
Proverbs 29:15	*"The rod and reproof give wisdom: but a child left to himself bringeth his mother to shame."*
Proverbs 29:17, 18	*"Correct thy son, and he shall give thee rest; yea, he shall give delight unto thy soul. Where there is no vision, the people perish: but he that keepeth the law, happy is he."*

UNIT THREE

MAKING DAD
A HERO

1

THE BEST THING YOU CAN DO FOR YOUR CHILD

When Kenny was about 12, I expressed some concern to my dad about him. During that conversation, I told my dad that Kenny was "crazy" about his dad. My dad assured me that Kenny's being "crazy" about his dad was more important at this point in his life than anything else. This thought sobered

> SUBMISSION = "SEEKING TO PLEASE IN EVERYTHING I DO"

me because I was reminded that if Kenny was crazy about his dad, I would probably need to be the one to make it so. I realize that my husband can make himself a hero to our son without my help. However, I also realize that I most likely have the ability to knock that hero down a peg or two in Kenny's eyes.

This conversation with my dad turned my thoughts to a verse which my husband had showed me. *"And he shall turn the heart of the fathers to the children, and the heart of the children to their fathers, lest I come and smite the earth with a curse."* (Malachi 4:6) I believe that the best thing I can do for my children is to turn their hearts toward their father—even if that means turning their heart away from me. My children were so fond of my husband that if I had left him, our kids would most surely not have gone with me!

In the household in which I grew up, my father was the most important part of our home. My mother scheduled our time so that our lives revolved around his schedule and his ministry. My mother often took a back seat and stood in the shadows as we made a hero out of our dad. As a young girl, I remember a particular moment when I think that my heart probably left my body and was given to my dad. On that day, a Daddy's girl was born. I did all that I could from that time on to be an encouragement to my dad and to really know my dad. I believe that my mother's allowing me this privilege is perhaps the best thing she ever did for me. Marriage was not much of an adjustment for me because I was used to spoiling the head of the house.

Today, however, the average mother is turning her children's hearts **away** from their father. This is one reason why I do not watch modern television programs. **On most of these shows, the father is made to look like an idiot.** Truly, the hearts of the children have been turned away from the fathers, and truly we have been smitten with a curse. I believe that curse is homosexuality and AIDS. My husband and father both say that they have never counseled a homosexual who did not have a domineering mother and who did not hate his father. I do not wish to condemn those who have a loved one who is a homosexual, and yet these two common denominators are only two of three that have been found in their counseling experience.

I also believe there is another curse in our nation which is a result of our hearts being turned away from our fathers. That is **abortion.** Mothers wish to be as good as fathers. They wish to be able to run for president of the country and of the corporation just as their husbands can. There is only one thing which completely hinders a woman from accomplishing what a man accomplishes. That is the "inconvenience" of pregnancy and childbirth. I have no doubt that the "free choice" expressed by many of the women's rights activists of this country is just their way of trying to be as good as or better than men. I suppose just about every curse we have in America today, such as teen suicide, can point back to the breakdown of a mother's lack of willingness to make Dad the king of her children's heart.

We just don't seem to be able to understand that God created submission and the headship of the home to benefit **everyone** involved. I believe that submission is the best child-rearing tool a mother has. Because of this, allow me to give you some ideas about how to turn your children's hearts toward their father.

1.   **Be willing to take second place.** I Peter 3:4 says that ladies are to adorn themselves with a meek and quiet spirit. Being quiet does not mean that we do not speak above a whisper. Being quiet means that we do not demand our own rights; rather, we are willing to take second place. The following are some ways to be number two:

A.   Encourage your kids to be close to their dad.

B.   Plan special activities rather than being negative and critical when Dad is busy. This will prevent preachers' kids from being sour about the ministry.

C.   Respond to his arrivals and departures to and from home.

D.   Wave to Dad as he drives away until he is out of sight. This is usually practiced in our home.

E.   Have the kids greet him at the door with his favorite snack or with his favorite newspaper. The dad of our home loves *USA Today*.

F.   Have the kids make him breakfast in bed.

G.   Have the kids give him back rubs.

H.   Have the kids bring him his favorite drink in bed.

I.   Respect his privacy and need to rest.

J.   Encourage your kids to run errands with him.

K.   Make signs for him.

L.   Change your schedule to eat meals with him.

M.   Repeat anything good Dad says about his children.

2.   **Be willing to honor Dad.** The following are some ways to honor him:

A.   Brag on him.

B.   Call him into the room, so you and your children can give him a standing ovation.

C.   Stand up for him as his defender to the children.

D.   Cover for him.

E.   Take the blame for him. This is very Christlike as Jesus took the blame for us.

I present this information not as that which I have followed as a perfect example. I present this as something I have tried to follow and as something which was followed to a great degree in my childhood.

Let me close by saying, "Hip, hip, hooray for dads"—especially for my dad who watches from Heaven and for the father of my children. Fathers are, after all, the most important people in our lives.

2

WHAT THE BIBLE DOESN'T SAY ABOUT CHILD REARING

Many women devote their lives to the cause of child rearing, making this their first priority in life. Perhaps their husbands are unsaved or backslidden. More commonly, the woman may be disenchanted with her husband or with the quality of her marriage. Therefore, the wife may devote the most quality and the most quantity of her time to rearing and training her children.

It was brought to my attention recently that there are **no** commandments in the relationship chapters of the Bible addressed to mothers. There are commandments to children, to fathers, to servants, to masters, to individuals, and to churches. But there are no commandments to mothers, only to wives.

The Bible **does** command us to train our children, particularly in the Old Testament. Because of the absence of commandments to mothers, I am led to believe that God intended most of the training to be done by the father. There is much instruction given to fathers and children, particularly in the book of Proverbs. However, the New Testament only gives one commandment to fathers: *"And, ye fathers, provoke not your children to wrath: but bring them up in the nurture and admonition of the Lord."* (Ephesians 6:4)

A similar commandment in Colossians 3:21 says, *"Fathers, provoke not your children to anger, lest they be discouraged."* From this command-ment and from the absence of commandments given to mothers, I again conclude that fathers are to train their children. I realize that there are many things that a mother can and should do for her children. She should nurture and care for them; she should love them. But she should not take the spiritual leadership of the home by training her children *"in the nurture and admonition of the Lord."* I have taught the young ladies in my marriage classes that it is the husband's responsibility to teach the children the Bible, and it is primarily the wife's responsibility to teach her children how to work.

So what if your husband won't teach the Bible to his children? Is it then necessary for you to become the Bible teacher or trainer of the home? Actually, I think the Bible teaches us a better way.

A Mother's Commands for Rearing Good Children

1. Submit yourselves unto your own husband. Ephesians 5:22, *"Wives, submit yourselves unto your own husbands, as unto the Lord."* The preceding verse, Ephesians 5:21, is a great complement to this. *"Submitting yourselves one to another in the fear of God."* I believe God intended a good Biblical marriage to be the tool He would use to train children. Children who see a good marriage see Bible principles come to life. They also see a three-dimensional picture of the love that God has for them. When a child sees his parents submitting to each other, he learns firsthand the advantages of living an obedient Christian life. The command for submission is addressed primarily to the wife, just as the commands for training children are addressed primarily to the father.

2. Seek to please your own husband. Proverbs 31:11, 12, *"The heart of her husband doth safely trust in her, so that he shall have no need of spoil. She will do him good and not evil all the days of her life."* I believe that Proverbs 31 is mainly teaching us all of the different ways that a virtu-ous woman seeks to please her husband. Again, when a child watches his mother continuously seeking to please her husband, he doesn't read or hear Bible commands; he sees them in action.

3. **Reverence your own husband.** Ephesians 5:33, *"...and the wife see that she reverence her husband."* The word "reverence" means "to honor with respect." Herein, I believe, lies the primary child-rearing command to mothers: **WIVES, MAKE A HERO OUT OF YOUR HUSBAND!** I did not say make a hero out of the neighbor's husband, the man at church, the grandfather, or the pastor. These may be good ideas, but they do not take the place of making a hero out of your husband!

How does following this command rear good children?

A. It motivates the father. I have been blessed to have a few people make me feel like a hero through the years, and believe me, it didn't make me want to walk all over them. It humbled me, it increased my capacity to love those people, and it made me feel responsible. When a mother and her children make a hero out of the father, it motivates him to want to lead and to train and to love as Christ loved the church. The idea that men walk all over women who treat them like heroes came straight from the world and the Devil; remember, the Devil is a liar and the father of lies.

B. It turns the hearts of the children to their true God-appointed trainer. Making a hero out of Dad causes children to respect their father. It causes the father-child relationship not to be a wrathful relationship, but a buddy relationship. When Dad is made a hero, it is easier for him to obey his only New Testament command regarding children, Ephesians 6:4 which says, *"And, ye fathers, provoke not your children to wrath: but bring them up in the nurture and admonition of the Lord."*

C. It rears good children by teaching them how to respond to their Heavenly Father. They learn to respond to God with obedience, fear, honor, praise, and love. In other words, they learn how to be good Christians and how to "turn out right."

D. It brings great joy to the mother. I am ashamed to admit that a few times in my life, I have not thought I got a fair deal in my marriage. You may be surprised that a wife would feel that way when her husband is Dr. Jack Schaap. This goes to prove that most of the time the feeling that we have been slighted in marriage is a result of our own sinful attitude. Luckily for me, I looked into the Bible and found that the problem was where it usually is—in the heart—my heart.

Then I set about to make a hero out of my husband. Because I married a great man and because I have treated my husband with honor and respect all of these years, I truly worship the ground upon which he walks. I am like a silly school girl; I am that excited about the privilege of being married to my husband. And the more excited I get about my husband, the more excited I get about God. These relationships are almost inseparably connected.

Ladies, 90 percent of you would adore your husband if you treated him like a hero! You would live your life each day thrilled with your husband—even more so than you did when you were dating him. Many of you, however, are miserable in a marriage from which you have no Biblical right to escape because you are only tolerating your husband. Pardon me for saying so, but that is not too smart!

Perhaps you feel that it will be worth it if your children turn out right, so you are busying yourself in training your children. But according to the Bible, you have the cart before the horse, and I'm afraid the cart and the horse are both going to crash!

Believe me, I am not trying to judge or condemn those of you who suffer with an unhappy marriage. Yet I do believe that many unsaved husbands would become Christians, many backslidden husbands would get right with God, and many hardened husbands would become loving ones. On the outside chance that yours might be the marriage that could be saved, I share my heart with all of you. In the next chapter, I am including a list of ways to help your children honor their father. If your marriage is troubled and you have not tried everything on the list, you have not done everything you can do. And if you have not done everything you can do to obey the Bible, you cannot be sure your children are being trained Biblically.

Please try everything on the list. You may have to try them again, and again, and again to soften the heart of your husband. You may never soften his heart, but I promise you will receive the blessing of God immediately, and you will be living true New Testament Christianity before your children. If you make a hero out of your husband, I guarantee you will be glad you did!

3

IDEAS FOR HONORING DAD

1. Get a list of his favorites— drink, pop, candy bar, snack, and so forth.

2. Have your child meet him at the door with one of his favorites.

3. Show up at an unexpected time and/or place with one of his favorites.

4. Put up a sign honoring Dad.

5. Decorate Dad's office door.

6. Call Dad into the room and give him a standing ovation.

7. Make Dad breakfast in bed.

8. Give Dad a back massage.

9. Give Dad a hand massage.

10. Give Dad a foot massage.

11. Have your child run errands with Dad.

12. Tell your child specific praise his dad has spoken about him.

13. Tell your child how much his dad loves him.

14. Have your child make a list of ten things he likes about Dad and have him share them one at a time.

15. Bake for Dad.

16. Make a praise box for Dad with a different line of praise for each day of the month so he can read one a day for a month.

17. Plan a picnic at Dad's place of work when Dad is extra busy.

18. Help Dad on special projects at work.

19. Attend special activities with Dad.

20. Send notes or cards to Dad and put them in unexpected places.

21. Cook Dad's favorite meal.

22. Refer your child's question to Dad; have your child go to Dad for advice.

23. Give Dad a funny cartoon.

24. Write Dad a poem.

25. Be thoughtful of Dad on special days such as Father's Day.

26. Send Dad an e-mail or a text message.

27. Send Dad a balloon bouquet.

28. Never criticize Dad.

29. Help other family members to be close to Dad.

30. Pray together for Dad.

31. Accept Dad's teasing.

32. Share jokes with Dad.

33. Plan what you will say to Dad when you see him.

34. Adapt to Dad's moods; do not expect him to adapt to yours.

35. Have your child brag on Dad in front of his friends and in Dad's presence.

36. Tell Dad how handsome, young, and strong he is.

37. Call Dad at work or from an activity.

38. Hug and kiss Dad.

39. Look Dad in the eye when you talk to him.

40. Ask Dad to tell you about his day.

41. Make Dad a card.

42. Make Dad a candy poster.

43. Go soul winning with Dad.

44. If Dad is a pastor, put a note and candy on his chair on the platform.

45. Leave a note in Dad's car.

4

TEACHING YOUR CHILD TO RESPECT OTHERS

The tool for teaching a child to respect others is the marriage relationship between the mother and father. Every parent wants his child to grow up to treat other people properly. No parent wants his child to be one who is the bully of the classroom and cannot get along with other students. I'm sure there is not a parent who sets out with a goal that his baby will become a problem to society. Many of those same parents who want their children to get along with others fail to see the importance of getting along with their spouse.

Titus 2:4, 5, *"That they may teach the young women to be sober, to love their husbands, to love their children, To be discreet, chaste, keepers at home, good, obedient to their own husbands, **that the word of God be not blasphemed."*** One of the meanings of the word *blaspheme* is "to think you know more than something." Who will think they know more than the Word of God? Those young children who have not been taught the things listed in Titus 2. Children who do not see the example of a husband's love and a wife's submission in marriage will not believe that the Bible has the answers for them.

Though all of these lessons listed in Titus 2 are critical, I want to bring out three words from these passages, not only for the teaching of the respect of God's word, but also for the teaching of respect for others. These three words are marriage, submission, and husband. The proper handling of these three subjects are of utmost importance in teaching a child to respect others. The relationship your children see in your marriage will be a pattern for all of their relationships. In addition to that, your children will probably love their spouse the way that they see you love yours. Therefore, your own good marital relationship is the best gift you can give your child. This whole idea is complicated, however, when we understand the truth that children themselves put a great deal of pressure on a marriage.

The following are some ideas that we used to show our children a happy marriage in spite of many pressures.

1. **Have a date with your spouse each week.** From the first year of our marriage until now, my husband and I have gone out on a date once a week.

2. **Don't be afraid to use baby sitters.** I did not leave our children much when they were small. Yet, when they were only two weeks old, I began to use baby sitters for two reasons: for a weekly, scheduled soul-winning time and for a weekly, scheduled date with my spouse.

I made sure that the baby sitters were competent. We once stopped using a baby sitter because she mentioned that she had read an entire book while we were away for the evening. Our children mentioned that they had gotten themselves their own supper while the baby sitter was reading. We replaced this baby sitter with one who made every evening a happening. She thoroughly planned each evening. To this day, our children love Mrs. Arischa Akin, and she loves them dearly. We were choosy about who baby-sat and about how often they baby-sat, but we were not afraid to use baby sitters. We knew that the marriage came first in our home, and that concept was very vital in the rearing of happy, respectful children.

3. **Ask the baby sitter to have your children in bed before you return home.** My husband and I needed a night to be just sweethearts. Not being parents from about 6:00 p.m. on Friday evening until Saturday morning made that possible.

4. **Teach your children that you desire each other's company.** At some point in their early childhood, I got down on my knees and told Jaclynn and Kenny that "sometimes Mommy and Daddy like to be all

alone, and they don't want anyone else to be with them." I would thoroughly explain to them how long we would be gone, and we went away at the same scheduled time every week.

5. Build your life around your husband, not around your children. This philosophy causes security in the hearts of your children. We made our marriage the center of our home. We demonstrated this in many ways; one way was by never allowing the children to sit between us in the car or in church. In a physical way, we showed our children that the marriage was the center of our home.

6. Find every opportunity to say positive things about your spouse. I made it a habit to brag on my husband to our children and never to criticize him. Remember the two rules of praise and incorporate them into your marriage.

    A. Never say anything negative about your husband.

    B. Take every opportunity to say something positive about your husband.

7. Don't tease about or criticize your spouse's ability with the children. When my husband was a teenager, his sister Kristi had serious health problems. She spent much time in the hospital, and her husband Roger spent most of that time with her. My husband's parents became the caretakers of Roger and Kristi's baby Tami. My husband learned how to care for a baby and had more experience with children than I did when our oldest was born. Because of this, my husband and I shared every aspect of child care together. I did not demand this. My husband just volunteered, and I made sure that I always made him feel that his child care was more than adequate. I knew that the more we had in common, especially with our children, the closer our marriage would stay during the pressured child-rearing years.

8. Cover your spouse's weaknesses. I remember several times when I was "reaching my limit" in child care or housework, my husband would take our children to another room, and I would hear him talking to them. "Mommy is tired; she works so hard." He could have looked at me and asked, "What is your problem? Why are you being such a jerk?" He perhaps would have been justified in saying I was acting like a jerk. But such statements and attitudes do not fit into a marriage where respect is a goal. It is especially not appropriate in a home where little children are looking and listening. And do not kid yourself, parents— they are looking and listening, and they do know when there is disrespect in the home.

My husband does not tend to be absent-minded, and he rarely makes mistakes. Yet, I remember more than once taking the blame before others for absent-minded mistakes that my husband made. I did not always handle such mistakes right initially, but before a frustration could become an argument, I took the blame. This type of covering for each other created a deep respect and a friendship between my husband and me that has passed on to our children.

9. **Show your excitement and your affection for your spouse.** I do believe in kissing and hugging in front of your children. Not being able to show affection puts unnecessary pressure on the marriage. Of course, I do not believe in performing intimate gestures before your children. I fear too many couples act "straight-laced" before their children. There is no hugging or kissing. Things like this cause the dull and pressured marriage to dissolve. Many times the same parent who was unaffectionate with his spouse will bring a boyfriend or girlfriend into the home and carelessly show intimacy before the children. This scenario is almost too sad to address, but I counsel with young adults regularly who still struggle with the insecurities caused by such atrocities' being committed in their home. I often wonder why those who commit such reckless behavior in an illicit affair could not have instead chosen to enjoy the spouse to whom they made their vows and with whom they had children.

Not only should you show your affection for your spouse, but you should also show your excitement for your spouse. I remember telling Jaclynn and Kenny that I wanted them to be excited when Daddy came home from work, then being disappointed sometimes when they weren't. I remembered that CHILDREN LEARN BY ACTION RATHER THAN BY WORDS. I decided that I would show excitement when my husband came home from work, and our children then followed my example.

10. **Teach your children God's order of authority.** The Bible

makes it clear that the father is the head of the wife. Ephesians 5:23a says, *"For the husband is the head of the wife."* I wanted our children to see this fact clearly. When Kenny was about seven, he said, "Mom, Dad is the boss of our home."

I answered, "I know."

He continued, "And someday I will be the boss of my home."

I answered, "That is right."

He finished, "And you'll never be the boss!"

To which I added, "That's okay because I like the boss I have."

When Kenny was in second grade, he was given a blank sheet of paper and this assignment: Write one complete sentence and draw a picture to go with it.

Kenny could write anything, as long as it was a complete sentence. Kenny's one complete sentence was, "My Dad is the boss!" He drew a picture of his father. I saved that picture, and I still have it. It was my hope that Kenny would still be able to write that sentence honestly when he was a teenager and an adult.

When Kenny graduated from high school, he wrote me a letter in which he thanked me for "always pointing me to God and to Dad." I saved that letter also, and I rejoiced that Kenny believed that to be true.

God teaches that the recipe for a happy home is:

(1) The husband to be the head of the wife

(2) The children to obey their parents.

When the first part of the recipe is not followed properly, it is hard to expect the second part to be carried out. When we leave an ingredient out of any recipe, we bring forth a damaged product. A chocolate chip cookie without chocolate chips is not going to turn out right, regardless of how many other right ingredients we put in it. So it is with child rearing. When the ingredients of submission and authority are missing, the child will turn out to be somewhat warped.

11. Never argue on child rearing in front of the children. This is a challenge, especially as the children become teenagers, but it is vitally important. Setting up guidelines ahead of time such as those mentioned in a previous chapter will help. Because I was with our children most of the day, my husband would come home unaware of our schedules. He might come home and spank the child when I knew the child was cranky because I had shopped all day and failed to give him a nap. The tendency was for me to be a "know-it-all" parent. "I always knew what was best for the children, and their father couldn't possibly know. Why he was hardly ever even home!" I put this in quotes because it was fictitious and not truthful.

The truth was, I could see that I was doing more damage by undermining my children's father through my attitude. I made a decision to live by this premise. IT IS BETTER FOR A CHILD TO BE UNJUSTLY PUNISHED BY HIS FATHER THAN IT IS FOR A CHILD TO SEE HIS FATHER'S AUTHORITY PUT DOWN IN ANY WAY.

This is true with any authority. Looking back, I remember times when I felt our children were treated unjustly by their father and by other authorities. I decided to at the very least keep my mouth shut and to give the authority the benefit of the doubt. I decided to believe that the other authorities in our children's lives were, like myself, trying their best to do what they thought was best. I do not regret taking this stand with authority. Our children are in their early 20s now. They love me, they adore their father, and they do not have problems with the authorities in their lives.

12. Don't come between your spouse and your children. One way we avoid this is by defending our spouse's disciplinary actions. Occasionally our children would complain to me about their father's actions or punishment. They did not do this often because they truly respected their father and our marriage. I rose to my husband's defense in such cases. Usually, the defense was mild and lighthearted because that was all that was needed.

Once when our daughter was five years old, she sassed her father at the dinner table. I grabbed our daughter by the chin, spilled ice water all over the table, and I reprimanded her firmly, "DON'T EVER TALK TO YOUR FATHER THAT WAY AGAIN." I wanted to "nip it in the bud," so to speak. I don't ever remember Jaclynn sassing her father again. My husband could have handled the sassing himself, but in this case, I think it was most effective for Jaclynn to see her mother stand up for her father. My husband has expressed gratitude to me time and time again for that incident. It definitely built the respect and friendship in our marriage, which is important for our children to see. When our children were small, they would sometimes run to me for a hug after their dad had spanked them. I exhorted them to "hug your daddy first, and then I will be glad to hug you." I wanted them to be right with their father first before they hugged me. Many mothers criticize their husband's punishment without saying a critical word. A simple "COME TO MAMA, BABY" and a big hug can say to the children, "Your dad should not have punished you like he did." This is very unwise.

13. **Switch roles when Dad arrives home.** I wanted it to be obvious to our children that there was a switch of authority when Dad got home. Because of this, I referred all questions to my husband when he was at home. A simple question such as "Can I have a piece of candy?" was referred to Dad. This not only built Dad's authority in the eyes of the children, but it also gave me a chance to rest in that authority until Dad had to leave the home again. An emotional woman tires of the decision-making responsibility, and she does herself a favor when she lets it rest in someone else's care for a while.

14. **Yield in conflict.** If there was a conflict in our home over things such as where the thermostat should be set, I made a predetermined decision that our children would see me yield. To this day, I do not know how to set our thermostat. You may think that is stupid, but I think that is pretty smart. I am very happy and also well taken care of.

I realize that these points will bring many challenges to a marriage, especially where there are children and teens involved. I do not want you to think that I always did what was right in these situations. There were a lot of mistakes and a lot of trial and error and saying "I'm sorry." Yet I can honestly say that these were typically the standards that were lived in our home, and I have no regrets about any of them.

The following list contains other points about teaching your child to respect others.

15. Don't be a respecter of persons. Acts 10:34 says, *"…God is no respecter of persons."* I believe this is one of the best lessons my parents lived before me. One of the best ways to cripple a child both spiritually and emotionally is to teach him that he is better than someone else. As a pastor's wife of a megachurch, I would be severely handicapped if I had not learned to avoid prejudice. My father went to Heaven five years ago, and I have been a pastor's wife for almost five years. One of the lessons that my father taught me and lived before me that has helped me the most these five years is "God is no respecter of persons."

16. Serve the Lord together. When Jaclynn was eight years old, she and my husband took over a bus route of just a few people and built it to several hundred. A few years later our son and I became involved on the bus route also. We won many souls to Christ and brought thousands of people to church. We also provided activities, Bible studies, gifts, money, medicine, and clothes for these people. Our children saw the other side of the billboards which advertise such things as cigarettes and alcohol. They saw the other side of immorality.

They brought children to church who were dirty and hungry because their mother had not gotten up and dressed them. Their mother had been too drunk to awaken and had been sleeping with her latest boyfriend. Our children walked into roach-infested apartments and onto floors laden with mounds of beer cans and trash. They learned to respect the person who most needed someone to respect him. They learned to love the person who could do nothing for them in return.

One mother came to me concerned because so many people tell her daughter how beautiful she is. "Will she become vain and think she is better than others?" this mother asked. The same mother expressed concern because her small daughter was infatuated with fairy tales such as Cinderella. "Mrs. Schaap," she asked, "Will this cause beauty to become too important to our daughter?"

In answer to this godly mother's questions, I said something like this. I DO NOT BELIEVE IT IS OUR JOB TO HUMBLE OUR CHILDREN. LIFE WILL HUMBLE THEM. The well-intentioned mistakes of good authorities will humble them. We will make our children proud if we run to those authorities and belittle those authorities for their good intentions and in spite of their diligent efforts. Life will humble our children; yet sadly, I think it is the belief of many parents that we are to humble them.

Our job is to build our children. Yes, our job is to punish, to train, to schedule and to pray, but it is not to criticize. Our job is to praise and to love. I often tell my daughter, daughter-in-law, and granddaughter how beautiful they are. I am passing on the legacy of my father. He often told me I was beautiful, but this did not make me feel I was beautiful as much as it made me feel that my father liked me. It made me feel that my father was wonderful! All around us are opportunities to teach our children humility. Those opportunities are found in people—people who disappoint us and people who need our help and can give us nothing in return.

One year at a Mother-Daughter banquet, Jaclynn and I sat near a little girl who had been badly burned. Her face was severely deformed, and I was concerned what four-year-old Jaclynn would say to the girl. She enjoyed the girl's company and said nothing unkind to her. On the way home, I asked Jaclynn, "What did you think of the way the little girl looked?"

Jaclynn answered, "She was pretty, Mom!" I was convicted by my daughter's answer. I realized I had a little girl under my authority who was well on her way to respecting others. I prayed I would do nothing by my own foolish pride that would change that fact.

Unit Four

Training
Kings and Queens

1

MAKING GOD REAL TO YOUR CHILDREN

When I was a teenager, my father wisely taught me that there are two types of parents who are spiritually impractical.

A. **The Spooky Parent.** This is the type of parent who is so spiritually minded that he is of no earthly good. This parent fails to show his children how God relates to their own childish interests.

B. **The Worldly Parent.** This type of parent puts God into a corner of his life but does not include God in all of his schedule. An example of this would be a parent who attends church on Sunday but does not do what the preacher preaches on Monday through Saturday.

The goal is for a parent to be balanced so that he can easily bring the reality of God into his children's world. The following are ideas that, when implemented, will make this possible.

1. **Stay in church.** Any time we have a change in our life, such as the birth of a new baby, it is easy to backslide from church attendance. There is a temptation to say that the church nursery is not good enough for our child. Babies do get sick frequently, and I do not believe in bringing a sick baby to church. On the other hand, if a parent is not careful, he will get used to staying at home from church because of his child's frequent sickness, and he will keep the child home unnecessarily.

When our children were small, we lived by this philosophy: "When in doubt, do go to church." If we knew our child was sick enough to stay home, we kept him home. If we were in doubt as to whether or not our children should stay home, we went to church. I do not believe our children were harmed from this, but rather they were helped by it. Our children grew up attending a church that has been labeled the "World's Largest Sunday School"; therefore, I suppose our children were sent every Sunday to one of largest nurseries in the world. Yet our children hardly ever got sick. I believe one reason is that the Lord honored our decision of "When in doubt, do go to church."

Most children do go through a stage, usually between the ages of nine months to two years, where they are sick a lot, and ours were no exception. Another thing we did to stay in church during this time was to make sure that only one of us stayed home with a sick child. It would have been a lot easier to stay home if my husband had also stayed home; however, because I had to stay home from church without him, I felt that I had missed even more by not being in church.

2. **Let your children see you in your devotional time.** I often saw my mom reading the Bible at the kitchen table when I was leaving to go to school. It was evident that God was very real to both of my parents. My husband frequently mentions seeing his dad reading his Bible at the kitchen table every morning when he was growing up.

Kenny recently wrote me a letter and mentioned how he had noticed his dad's and my faithfulness to our Bibles. It was not unusual for Kenny to come down the stairs in the morning and find his dad reading his Bible at the kitchen table, while I was reading mine on the living room couch. Sometimes Kenny would even catch us on our knees in prayer. This is one of the memories he thanked us for when he prepared to leave our home for marriage.

3. **Give God the credit for the special things that happen in your lives.** Several years ago I started the habit of asking God to show Himself to me each day and then writing down in a daily journal one way that He did. I have shared several of these things with our children.

I had a hummingbird feeder in our yard for a year or two and never saw a hummingbird. On a trip to Colorado, we noticed several hummingbirds coming to a feeder at the office of the condominiums where we were staying. My husband and I decided to purchase a feeder and hang it on the deck of our condominium. Every morning we would read our Bible on the deck and watch the hummingbirds. We took about 40 pictures of hummingbirds on our vacation. Our children teased us that we took many more pictures of hummingbirds than we did of them. Remember that I had not had a hummingbird at my home feeder all year…

We arrived home from Colorado on a Saturday evening. I got up quite early Sunday morning, around 5:30 a.m. When I looked out my window, I discovered a hummingbird flying around our porch. That hummingbird stayed around our porch all day long, and then we never saw it again. It was almost as if one had gotten stuck in our suitcase and flown back with us. Our whole family saw the hummingbird, or else even I would feel like I was making the story up. Our children know that a hummingbird is one of the things I look for to show me that God loves me. They knew that God sent the hummingbird to encourage a weary pastor and pastor's wife who had just arrived back from their first vacation since taking on a huge ministry.

When traveling in Tennessee, our family was hoping to see some black bears. We asked a park ranger what the likelihood was that we would see some. "Actually," he said, "it is very rare to see a black bear here." We prayed and asked the Lord to help us see a black bear. Barely five minutes after we left the park ranger, we saw not just one black bear but a mother black bear and her two cubs.

I can't begin to tell you all of the stories of souls won. We prayed for our neighbors to be saved. One evening we woke up in the middle of the night and found our neighbors' house on fire. My husband was able to put out the fire before the fire department even got there. The next day we were able to lead Pat and Bill Tabor to the Lord. Eventually, the whole family was saved: Pat, Bill and their two children, Matthew and Katie.

I share most of these stories with our children. Many of them I do not have to share. They have seen them firsthand. Often they tease me, "Mom and her stories…." I don't know if they think I am a good mother or not, but I believe our children know that God is real.

4.   Don't just talk about the Lord at family altar. Bring Him up at the most enjoyable times. Deuteronomy 6:7 says, *"And thou shalt teach them diligently unto thy children, and shalt talk of them when thou sittest in thine house, and when thou walkest by the way, and when thou liest down, and when thou risest up."* When you are asking God to show Himself to you each day, when you are seeking Him and walking with Him, it is not hard to talk about Him. I have ways that I look for God such as looking for hummingbirds. I am not trying to put God in a box by saying, "God, show me a black bear or a hummingbird." I am trying to give God ways to show off. When I see Him show off, it is very natural to tell my children about it wherever we happen to be at that time or whenever I see them next. I find that God likes to show off for us if we'll just give Him the glory for it. Children and teenagers enjoy seeing God at work in their lives and in the lives of their parents.

5.   Allow your spouse to balance you. Actually, when it came to rearing our children, I found myself to be very matter of fact. I found my style of teaching our young children the Bible to be boring and uninspiring. As I watched my husband's more spontaneous, fun-loving approach of training our children, I learned from it. At first, I found it to be abrasive to my more stern nature. Then I realized how foolish I was for wanting my husband to do things my way when my way wasn't really working. I decided to learn from my spouse, and I think he balanced me in my child rearing. I believe the balancing I received from learning from him made me a better representative of Christ before our children.

6.   Pray with them about little things that are important. To be honest, when our children were little, it was more important to pray with them about black bears than about saving America. Why? It was something to which they could relate. It was something that brought God to where they were. I learned to pray with our children about everything. We often prayed together as they did their homework, especially in the difficult tasks. We did a lot of praying as our children were going through the difficult task of learning how to read. I learned to take my prayer requests to our small children. They enjoyed my trust in them as my little prayer warriors.

I started praying with my children before they were even old enough to understand. Even now I pray with our 19-month-old granddaughter before she eats. I fold her pudgy hands, and we pray, "Dear Jesus, Thank you for bananas. Amen." We thank God for whatever food she is eating at that time.

7. **Praise them for their practical use of God's Word.** Praise them when you see them reading the Bible; praise them when you see them praying. Praise them when they win a soul. Praise them for doing right. Be sure you praise them over these things as much as you would over a report card with straight "A's."

8. **Make them spend at least some time each day in Bible reading and prayer.** When our children started elementary school, we made a short time of Bible reading and prayer a part of their morning schedule. Sometimes we read the Bible and prayed together around the dinner table or while on vacation, but we made it more of a priority to teach them to read the Bible and to pray alone.

One summer morning Kenny was headed out the door to play. He had on his baseball hat and was carrying a baseball bat, a baseball glove, and a baseball.

"Did you read your Bible this morning?" I asked as he approached the back door.

"No, ma'am," he answered.

"You have to read it before you go to play baseball."

I heard a deep sigh. I heard the bat, the ball, and the glove drop on the floor, and then I heard this question, "Where is the story of the giant that got killed?"

I gave Kenny the reference, and I wondered if he would ever learn to love the Bible, but my husband and I persisted. A **personal** walk with God is probably the most important thing that any person can learn.

9. **Make your standards consistent with those of your church.** Having inconsistent standards is the greatest sign of a worldly parent. I frequently talk to pastors' teenage and adult children who are turned off by their parents' standards because of witnessing their parents' double life. None of us are completely consistent, but it is important that we let people see who we really are so that our children do not get the idea

that we are living a lie. I don't mean that we have to let the people at church know if we just had an argument with our spouse. However, if arguments become the norm for our marriage, we should not try to portray a happy marriage publicly; rather, we should seek help from a pastor or Christian counselor to get healing for our marriage.

Be as kind and courteous at home as you are at church—again, so that your children will not notice a double standard. Also, if you are fun-loving and casual at home, don't put on pious "airs" when you enter the church building. Be what God wants you to be, what your family needs you to be, and then let people know who you really are.

If you make a grievous error, I am not saying the whole world has to know, but your fellow church members should know you to be what you are typically at home.

To the best of their ability, parents should find a church whose standards they believe and can follow. Then that family should follow those standards. When parents hear the pastor preaching that certain behavior is wrong and then go home and live contrary to that preaching, they are teaching spiritual inconsistency to their children. They are saying by their behavior, "God is good enough for Sundays, but He is not practical or real enough to be followed at home during every day of our lives." My father, Dr. Jack Hyles, used to say, "It is better to be in a church where the standards are lower and to follow every one of them than to be in a church with higher standards that the family does not follow at home." Of course, the best case scenario is to be in a church with high standards and to follow them at home.

10. Support the authorities in your children's lives. When another authority, such as a youth director or a Christian school teacher, mistreats your child and you as a parent become angry, you send an inconsistent signal about God to your child. You are saying, "God is love, but His love is not real enough or practical enough to handle the everyday irritations of our lives."

Most of the authorities in our children's lives treated them beautifully. Jaclynn and Kenny had the finest of school teachers, and I am so thankful for the youth director they both had, Dr. Eddie Lapina. He not only loved our children, he had a vision for them. I do remember at least one time thinking that another authority had mistreated our children. I kept my mouth shut and prayed about it.

It takes a group of people to rear good children. When the parents become angry at every authority with which they disagree, they cut apart their child's support group so that instead of having several leaders pulling on the same rope, they only have a few. The child's respect for authority becomes conditional. He learns to evaluate everything he is told by authority and to follow it only if he believes it to be right in his own eyes. This, in its final end, leads to rebellion and anarchy.

Sometimes a teenager or young adult may become at odds with his parents. The only hope that child might have to turn out right is if he can relate with some authority who will support the training of the parents. If the child is not connected by respect with the other authorities in his life, such as the pastor, he will not have anyone else to help him reconcile with his parents. The other links in the chain that are pulling him toward righteousness will be broken.

11.   Don't set convictions or preferences without Biblical principles and prayer. Some parents rear their children with an attitude of pride. Their insecure ego causes them to need to feel that others recognize that their child is superior to other children. I have known some parents that would not allow their children to socialize with other Christian friends over trivial matters. There are times when wise parents will isolate their child from the wrong crowd and from harmful behavior. However, some parents isolate their children from their Christian peers unnecessarily. Do not force your child to be different from his peers just for the sake of being different.

A child should be separated from his peers only after much prayer on the parent's part. When this happens, much wisdom should be used by the parent as he explains to his child the Biblical principle behind the separation. If at all possible, the child should then be pointed toward other good, Christian peers. A Christianity that isolates from all others in order to feel superior is an impractical Christianity which teaches an unloving and impractical image of God.

Children are basically social creatures, especially teenagers. To the best of our ability, we should provide our children with a good social

environment. Often it is our lack of prayer and faith in God which causes us to overprotect our children. We not only protect them from the
wrong crowd; we overprotect them from the right crowd.

A parent should train his child when he is young about how to
make decisions. Then he will have to let go some while the child is a
teenager, giving him a chance to practice making decisions while he is
still under his parents' roof. This is the best time to learn. It is a time
when the consequences of wrong are not as great.

May I add to this that when a child or teenager comes to his parents and asks, "What is wrong with that?" the wise parent will patiently look his child in the eye and explain from the Bible just what is wrong
with "that." He will not become angry with the child, even if the child
asks the same question 100 times.

I was one of those children who questioned standards over and over.
My father patiently told me more than once what was wrong with the
things that I questioned. So did my mother. I'm glad I did not hide my
disagreements with my parents' standards. I openly and honestly discussed them. By the time I was an adult, I knew what I believed not
because my parents believed it, but because I believed it.

**12. Rear your child for their sake and not for the sake of other
people.** Many parents, especially full-time Christian workers, make the
mistake of letting their reputation become an issue in their child rearing. This type of parent will correct his child publicly and force his child
to perform before others. He will tend to blame others when his child
does wrong. After yelling at someone else because "it is not my child's
fault," the same parent will go home and lose his temper with his child.
"What will people think? You know I am a deacon in the church" is an
example of what such a parent might say.

I made it a goal not to worry about my reputation with our children.
I have never heard my husband mention his reputation to our children,
even when they went through difficult times—and they did, by the way.
Our emphasis was always on doing what was best for our children.

I let our children be silly when they were small. I remembered a
statement made by my Child Psychology teacher from Hyles-Anderson
College, Mrs. Frieda Cowling:

"Children are children.
Children act like children.
Much of childish behavior is unpleasant."

I did not jump on our children's every mistake; I let them be children. As they became teenagers, they would occasionally wear something or do something that I knew would draw criticism from others. But if it was not a rule that my husband and I had set and it did not conflict with the Bible, we let them do things differently than our personal taste or choice would dictate. Why? Because our children were more important to us than our reputation.

CONCLUSION

When Jaclynn was a little girl, we had four chairs around our dining room table. I told her that one chair was for Daddy, one for Mommy, one for Jaclynn, and the other was for Jesus. Jaclynn's childlike faith accepted the reality of Jesus very quickly. In fact, when we had company one evening, she told a lady guest that she was sitting on Jesus.

Recently, while I was out to lunch with Jaclynn, I told her about a young lady in our church who was having difficulty in her pregnancy. "Mom, could we pray for her right now in the restaurant?" Jaclynn asked. We prayed for her right then.

A few weeks ago my husband and I stayed in a five-bedroom home with our children and grandchild for four days as we visited Disney World together. Each morning my husband and I got up and sat on the patio by the pool and read our Bibles. We noticed that Jaclynn did the same each morning.

When Kenny was about two, I told him that God was everywhere and that "He is right here with us."

Kenny responded, "No, He's not; I don't see Him." (The male gender has a little bit more trouble accepting things by feeling and not by sight.) I was a little concerned about Kenny's faith in God at the time, but I am not now. Last year he wrote me a letter in which he thanked me for always pointing him to God and Dad and not to myself. As I wrote earlier, I do not know if our children would tell you I am a good mother or not, but I know they would tell you that God is real to them and to their parents.

I was extremely close to my father. He is the human most responsible for making God real to me. My father obviously walked very close to God, as did my mother. God was very real in our home.

My father has been in Heaven for five years at the time of this writing. Has his absence shaken my faith? No! Though I miss my father, his absence has not really even shaken my joy. Why? Because my father gave me something when I was just a little girl that he knew would carry me through anything. He passed down from his mother the reality of faith in God.

I wanted my own children to receive the same from me. I wanted to give them something that would carry them through whatever trials life might hand them. There is not any material thing or any amount of money that can perform this task. One of the priorities of my parenting was to pass on what I had been given by my parents and my grandmother before me. I wanted to pass on the reality of faith in God. I believe that should I go to Heaven before them and should I never again be able to buy them a material gift or to bless them with my loving presence, our children will be okay. I am sure they will miss me, but they will be okay. Why? Because they had a great mom who didn't make mistakes? No, because they know the reality of faith in a God Who loves them and Who is all they need.

2

TEACHING TITUS TO OUR DAUGHTERS

"The aged women likewise, that they be in behaviour as becometh holiness, not false accusers, not given to much wine, teachers of good things. That they may teach the young women to be sober, to love their husbands, to love their children, To be discreet, chaste, keepers at home, good, obedient to their own husbands, that the word of God be not blasphemed." (Titus 2: 3, 4, 5)

A daughter needs to be taught that her self-esteem comes from doing things God's way. It comes from doing what God wants her to do, being what God wants her to be, and knowing what God wants her to know.

SELF-WORTH

My definition of self-worth is: the price your Creator was willing to pay for you. Self-worth cannot be changed. However, self-esteem or confidence is very changeable, sometimes from moment to moment. I believe that most young women today have very poor self-esteem. Why? Because they are looking for self-esteem in all of the wrong places. Many girls know how to spike a volleyball and dunk a basketball. Beware

> SELF-WORTH = THE PRICE YOUR CREATOR WAS WILLING TO PAY FOR YOU. SELF-WORTH CANNOT BE CHANGED.

of sending your daughter to even a Christian college that puts more emphasis on sports or careers than on marriage and motherhood.

Young women may know all about sex and beauty. But few daughters are being taught what God wants them to know, and self confidence comes from this.

Titus 2 gives us the only clear curriculum about what the aged woman (the mother) is supposed to teach the younger woman (the daughter). Of course, it doesn't have to be a mother teaching a daughter; it can be a teacher teaching a student. But in this chapter, we apply this subject to mothers and daughters.

1. A mother needs to teach her daughter how to be sober. The word *sober* doesn't just mean "not drunk." In this passage, it means "disciplined thinking." This verse implies that women are supposed to be taught to bring stability to a situation and to a home. Usually, it is just the opposite. Women are known to bring instability to their home.

A wise mother will teach her daughter to walk with God, for it is a walk with God that is the most fundamental way for a daughter to learn to be stable or sober in her thinking. A daughter needs to be taught how to handle depression Biblically and how to have a happy, consistent spirit.

2. A mother needs to teach her daughter how to love her husband. This is the discipline of affection. A mother cannot teach her daughter this if she divorces her husband. A mother who is disciplined in her thinking will be able to discipline herself to be moved with affection toward the same man for the rest of her life. A wise mother will teach her daughter to honor her father as a way of preparing the daughter to love her husband properly. The father is the key in teaching a daughter how to love her husband. Also, the items listed in the chapter "Love Is the Key" can be taught to a daughter, as well as displayed toward her.

3. A mother needs to teach her daughter how to love her children. This is the discipline of child rearing. The loving relationship between a mother and daughter is one of the best techniques for teaching a daughter to love her own children someday. Also, training your daughter to work with those who are less fortunate, such as poor children, can prepare her for motherhood. She needs to learn to love those who can give her nothing in return. Providing baby-sitting jobs is another way to train your daughter in this area.

Notice the sequence of God's curriculum. A woman who properly loves her husband will have an easier time loving her children properly without being unable to let go when they leave the nest.

4. A mother needs to teach her daughter how to be discreet. This is the discipline of minding her own business. The key element in teaching this is prayer. A mother should train her daughter to pray in personal devotions. A mother and daughter can bring heartaches to the Lord in prayer together. A mother should teach her daughter by example how to pray about differences with authority rather than speaking to an authority and trying to correct him.

5. A mother needs to teach her daughter how to be chaste. This is the discipline of purity. Setting standards is the key element in teaching a daughter to be pure. People who stay pure don't do so because their flesh is more sanctimonious than someone else's. They do it because of the standards and righteous habits they set for themselves. Don't be afraid of being too strict when you give your children standards and expect them to abide by them.

In sequence, a person who is discreet and minds his own business is also more likely to be pure. Getting outside of your own area and not minding your own business can lead to impurity.

6. A mother needs to teach her daughter how to be a keeper at home. This is the discipline of homemaking. The mother is the key element in this area. (See Part Three of Unit II entitled "Training Children" on page 69 for ideas.)

7. A mother needs to teach her daughter how to be good. This is the discipline of self-esteem and is best learned through a walk with God and by knowing what God wants us to know.

8. A mother needs to teach her daughter how to be obedient to her own husband. This is the discipline of submission. Authority is the key element in teaching this discipline. Teaching your daughter to obey the rules at school and of the teacher when she doesn't understand them is important. It is most important to teach your daughter how to obey her father's authority whether or not she understands it. The word *submission* means "a mission underneath" or "a mission behind the scenes." A daughter should be taught to spend a lot of time at home serving her father "behind the scenes."

Notice the words in Titus 2:5b, *"…that the word of God be not blasphemed."* One of the meanings of the word *blaspheme* is "to say something doesn't work." When our daughters are not taught how to do what God wants them to do, they will say that God's commands don't work. They will say they are not relevant for our lives in the twenty-first century. Does that sound familiar?

Titus 2:7a, *"In all things shewing thyself a pattern of good works…."* Not only are we to teach our daughters the virtues of Titus 2, but we are also supposed to possess them ourselves. Mothers are to say to their daughters, "Watch me, and I will show you how to perform the items listed in Titus 2." We are to show our daughters how to love and be obedient to their husbands by loving and being obedient to our own.

When our daughters see mothers who are depressed, impure in behavior, quick to correct and get angry at authority, lazy and sloppy in their housekeeping, and failing in their relationship with their husband, they will say, "The Word of God doesn't work. If Mom and Dad can't get along, why should we follow their spiritual principles? They can't even follow them."

We are to stand before our children as a pattern of these things. We can't be perfect as mothers, but we should not quit trying. We can't be superwoman, but through Christ, we can be a supernatural pattern!

3

REARING
FEMININE GIRLS

Several years ago the Arby's chain of fast food restaurants used this slogan: DIFFERENT IS GOOD! I am not sure how they were using this slogan, nor do I care to know, but I do believe that the Bible teaches us that God feels a similar way about most things. DIFFERENT IS GOOD!

God is not a one-world God. He does not like the nations to be united. In Genesis 11, some people tried to unite the nations of the world by building a tower to reach to Heaven, the Tower of Babel. God destroyed the tower and confounded the people so that they could not understand each other. Why? Because God believes that DIFFERENT IS GOOD!

In Ezekiel, God says that one of the reasons He destroys a nation is that the preachers of that nation do not teach that there is a **difference** between right and wrong. Ezekiel 22:26, *"Her priests have violated my law, and have profaned mine holy things: they have put no difference between the holy and profane, neither have they shewed difference between the unclean and the clean…."*

Genesis 1:27 teaches us that God intended men and women to be different. *"So God created man in his own image, in the image of God created he him; male and female created he them."*

God never makes mistakes, so he never made a girl and thought, "Uh-oh, I meant you to be a boy." Even if your husband always wanted a boy and you have five girls, God meant all five of them to be just that—feminine girls. And even if a mother has a son who has a softer nature than his brother and who has a hard time getting along with his father, God intended this mother to do her part to rear her son to be what God made him to be—a masculine man.

The following are some suggestions for rearing feminine girls.

1. Realize that femininity starts on the inside and works its way out. When I was a young girl, I didn't **feel** very feminine. Our church had a charm school for teenagers when I was in high school. Our teacher, a former model, had a difficult time teaching me how to swing my arms just right when I walked. I did not feel very feminine at charm school.

When our family had devotions, all of the girls prayed around one night, and the boys prayed around the next night. Because there were four girls and two boys, my two sisters and my mother prayed on girls' night, and my father, my brother, and I prayed on boys' night.

My mother is a tall, gracious, blonde Southern belle who seems to me to be naturally feminine. My sister, two years older than I, is tall and blond and resembles my mother. Both of my sisters are accomplished pianists. I took piano lessons for five years and can play two songs: "Mary Had a Little Lamb," and "Here We Go, Up a Row, to a Birthday Party." I did not feel very feminine as a child.

My mother, Beverly Hyles, has said that "Femininity is caring for others." I have known some gorgeous women who became hardened and masculine as they got older. Why? Because they learned to be feminine on the outside but not on the inside, and what we are on the inside eventually comes out.

I have also known some awkward tomboys who became very feminine ladies as adults. It is important to teach our girls to emphasize being feminine on the inside before we emphasize being feminine on the outside.

2. Teach your daughter that a girl was made for a completely DIFFERENT reason than a boy. Genesis 2:18, *"And the LORD God said, It is not good that the man should be alone; I will make him an help meet for him."*

There is one word in this passage that can summarize why the first girl was made and how we can teach our girls to be feminine on the inside. That one word is "help."

A man was made for a work. He was made to lead a home. His work may lead to public recognition and to applause and ovations, but a woman was made for a completely DIFFERENT reason. She was made to help.

As a pastor's wife and a former pastor's daughter, I have received more than my share of attention. I have received public recognition, applause, and ovations. I have taught classes, made speeches, and written books, but I keep my main focus on helping my husband. I do this not only because it is the reason I was made, but also because it is the thing that makes me the most happy and fulfilled. God knew what would make women happy, and He gave to them that purpose. He does not choose the man to lead because He likes men better, but rather because God knows what will make both the man and the woman the happiest.

3.   **Teach your girl from a very young age to help.** Teach her that helping is fun and that the men have the hard part of leadership. Because the man's work is so difficult, he needs someone to help him. The world has made the man's role look like fun and games when it isn't. Then it has made the woman's role look demeaning. No one can truly decide for us whether or not our role is big or little. We choose for ourselves whether to exalt or to put down our role.

Practice with your daughter saying the words, "May I help you?" Even the intonations of this phrase sound feminine. I practice with my Hyles-Anderson College students saying the words, "May I help you?" and they always say them with a soft, feminine lilt. They accent the last syllables of the sentence, which in itself gives a feminine sound. It is difficult to say, "May I help you?" in a deep, gruff voice.

I love helping my husband. Even though our children are grown and I work part-time outside the home, I choose to do all of my own housework and cooking. I choose to do this, though I could probably afford to hire help, because I love taking care of my husband and family. I love being a keeper at home.

I have seen ladies get gruff and hard as they age. They become bossy toward their husbands, and their husbands become more and more submissive. I don't think any young wife really wants that for her future, but young girls need to be taught that doesn't happen all at once. *We will be what we are becoming!*

2.   Teach your daughter to have a good attitude about the marriage relationship. If parents do not show a pattern of a happy marriage before their children, their children will not develop a good attitude toward marriage.

God invented marriage before the fall of man, and everything God invents is excellent in every way. Marriage is not only a God-ordained institution; it is the first God-ordained institution. Therefore, it is important and excellent! Marriage never fails; people fail. People mess up this wonderful plan of marriage. This sours the children of the failed marriages on God's excellent plan. Children from failed marriages will blaspheme the Word of God.

"That they may teach the young women to be sober, to love their husbands, to love their children, To be discreet, chaste, keepers at home, good, obedient to their own husbands, that the word of God be not blasphemed." (Titus 2:4, 5)

You can't say, "I hate marriage; marriage is the pits!" in a feminine voice. These words come out with a harsh tone of voice and a sour, hard expression. Girls who carry this ungodly attitude in their hearts toward marriage will become more masculine and less feminine as the years pass. They will be part of the blending of the sexes and will destroy the difference God intended.

Teach your daughter from a young age that:

    A.   God intended most girls to marry.

    B.   Marriage is excellent in every way.

    C.   You can look to your own parents for an example of a happy, godly marriage.

Then be sure that your life portrays that you really believe all of those things.

3.   Teach your daughter to pray daily for the man God has for her to marry. The very act of praying for her future husband to stay pure and safe will create a feminine heart in your daughter.

The members of the First Baptist Church of Hammond, Indiana, often thank me for choosing to marry my husband because he has made a wonderful pastor for them. He was groomed to take my father's place as pastor of our great church. Humanly speaking, if I had not married my husband, our church would not have had such a godly, prepared man when my father went to Heaven. I do remember clearly praying that God would lead me to the man He had for me to marry.

Two weeks before I met and started dating my husband, I spent a long season in prayer in our empty church auditorium praying for my future mate. At this time, I told God that I didn't want to marry the kind of man that I wanted to marry; I wanted to marry the kind of man that God wanted me to marry. God led me to both the man that He wanted for me and a mate that I very much wanted. Should I be thanked for finding my husband? Probably the people who should be thanked are people like my parents and teachers who taught me to pray for God to lead me to my husband.

4. **Teach your daughter to honor her father.** As alluded to earlier in this chapter, I did not always feel feminine as a young girl, but I was very close to my father. He convinced me that he not only loved me, but also liked me. I spent much time with him. I waited for him until late after church when he counseled after each service. I came home early from youth activities to spend time talking with him before he went to bed. I did things for him—I made him posters, homemade gifts, cards, etc. In unit 3, chapter 3 (page 111) I included a list of ideas of ways a girl can honor her father. Mothers can use this list to help their daughters to honor Dad. This will bring the mother and the daughter closer and reinforce the mother's respect for Dad also.

A girl who has a negative attitude toward her dad for any reason will not be a good wife, nor will she be feminine until she reconciles that attitude. A girl who honors her father is learning not only how to be a good wife but also how to be feminine.

5. **Teach your daughter to go into every situation seeking to serve.** Teenagers are often the least confident of humankind. Why? Because they tend to go into a situation seeking to identify with the

most popular. More often than not, this action fails, and the teenager's confidence is devastated. It is wise for a teenager to go into a situation asking, "Who needs my help?" Often, this person who needs help will be the least popular. This serving teenage girl (and adult) will have greater confidence and be more feminine.

6. **Teach your daughter not to be self-conscious.** It is vital that a girl learns femininity from the inside out so that she will learn not to be thinking of herself. The girl who is taught that femininity is just a method of walking, standing, and so forth will either be thinking of her charm and grace or defeated by her lack thereof.

Teach a girl to focus on helping others and making others feel better about themselves, perhaps by noticing some good quality about them. This will help her to forget about herself. There is no one as ugly or as unfeminine as the person who is consumed with self.

I used to be self-conscious when I was introduced as the daughter of my well-known father. When I learned to make eye contact with the person whom I was meeting and to try to make the person feel better about himself after having been with me, my self-consciousness went away.

7. **Teach your daughter to understand the advantages of being a lady.** My husband sometimes asks me if I want him to get the car for me—especially on a cold or rainy day. When he asks, I often reply with a grin, "You know I don't believe in women's rights!" There is advantage to disagreeing with this women's rights concept. The feminine woman understands the value of male chivalry.

8. **Teach your daughter not to be loud.** The Bible says in I Peter 3:4 that a woman should adorn herself with a meek and quiet spirit. Being meek means that a woman does not consider herself superior or inferior to anyone else. Being quiet in spirit doesn't mean that a woman never speaks above a whisper. Neither does it mean that a woman cannot cheer loudly at a ball game or where it is appropriate. It does mean, however, that a woman should not be heard from two miles away. A feminine woman should not be someone who has to draw the attention to herself by causing an interruption.

9. **Teach your daughter not to chase boys.** A girl should be

taught never to be aggressive toward a young man, especially in dating. Just because a girl has had one date with a man does not mean she has a right to pursue him. He should do all the pursuing. When the girl pursues a man in dating, she is leading the relationship and doing the opposite of being submissive. A girl should be taught never to boss a man or to be disrespectful to a man.

Even though I taught college men in my English classes at Hyles-Anderson College for several years, I did not tell them what to do. Rather, I told them what the administration said they were to do. Even though most of the men were many years younger than I was, I spoke to them with respect. I respected the fact that they were men, and I respected my own femininity too much to be bossy toward them. I supported the rules of the administration, but I was not bossy.

10. Don't allow your daughter to play with boys or touch boys. A girl who becomes too familiar with boys will not only be more likely to become a tomboy, but she also may be less interested in boys when she becomes of marrying age. It is vital that boys and girls keep their mystique around each other. We as parents need to help our children to keep this mystique. We did not invite boys to our daughter's birthday parties.

We also did not allow boys to baby-sit our children. We made this decision because of my husband's and my experience with counseling. More than one young man has confessed to fondling or sexually abusing a child when he was an adolescent who was asked to baby-sit. At this age, a boy's hormones are raging. Coupled with the fact that young boys tend to be much more curious than young girls, my husband and I made it a policy not to use male baby sitters. We were very choosy about our baby sitters altogether. Primarily, we used one older lady while I was working part-time, and we used the same college girl while we dated every Friday evening.

11. Don't allow your daughter to play organized sports. The Bible says the woman is to be a help meet in her marriage. I do not believe that a woman's playing basketball while her boyfriend is sitting on the bleachers cheering promotes femininity. I have watched organized women's basketball, and there is nothing feminine about it. I also believe that encouraging young men to sit on the side and cheer organized women's sports promotes a less masculine quality in the men.

12. Teach your daughter to be positive in her responses. Nothing is more unfeminine than negativity. A girl should practice saying the words, "Go for it!" Even if I disagree with my husband, I try to make my response to his ideas not deceitful, but still positive. I then pray about the matter.

A man who does not feel his opinions are valuable will refuse to share them. This leads to poor communication in marriage. A young lady needs to learn how to value the ideas and opinions of others so that she will know how to respond to her future husband.

13. Teach your daughter to do feminine chores. When our daughter was just a small girl, I taught her to clean the house, get the groceries, sew, cook, bake, garden, and so forth. Our son helped with some of these chores until he was 12, and we no longer allowed him to do feminine chores. Instead, we bought him a push lawn mower and put him in charge of all the outdoor chores.

14. Give your daughter feminine heroines. Teach her to honor the pastor's wife as well as the pastor and the youth director's wife as well as the youth director. This was something my husband and I stressed with our daughter. In high school Jaclynn and a couple of her friends took their youth director's wife out to lunch. She commented that this was the first time any of the teens in her youth group had taken her out to lunch. Your daughter needs lady heroines.

15. Demand strict obedience from your daughter. A boy should be taught to obey, but a girl should be taught to obey with a positive spirit.

16. Teach your daughter to sit, stand, walk, and talk like a lady. A lady should sit with her legs together. She should walk erectly while taking small, straightforward steps and gently swinging her arms. She should not walk harshly like a farmer, nor should she swing her hips like a harlot. She should learn to speak softly, yet professionally, with the opposite gender. She should learn to dress modestly. She should learn to look a man in the eyes only, to stand a proper distance away from a man, and to never follow a man with her eyes after he has passed her. In this day and age, if a mother does not teach her daughter these things, who will?

You may notice that I left all of the outward manifestations of femininity until the last point. Why? Because all of these will be in vain and will promote nothing more than self-consciousness if they are not proceeded by a feminine heart.

When Jaclynn was in junior high school, my husband and I watched her walking away from our car one day. Jaclynn was walking head first with her head kind of tilted down. "She walks funny," my husband said.

I replied, "I think she has the awkward junior high girl walk. I believe that when she meets the man she is supposed to marry, that walk will change."

Sure enough, when Jaclynn matured and fell in love, she developed all of the feminine charms, one of which is a gracious walk.

I am not opposed to teaching a girl how to walk like a lady, but I did not spend most of my time training Jaclynn in that area. I spent most of my training time teaching her to honor her father, to understand her supportive role as a female, and to care for others. I did not want Jaclynn to be self-conscious of her walk. I felt that a feminine attitude of caring for others would eventually bring about a feminine walk.

17. Teach your daughter how to dress like a lady. I interviewed both my husband and my father on the subject of ladies' dress, and I passed these points on to my daughter and continue to pass them on to the students I teach at Hyles-Anderson College.

    A. Fix your hair first thing each day. Don't wear a ponytail or your hair up in a "claw" two days in a row.

    B. Accent your waist in your dress. Wear your clothes tight enough to show you are a woman, but loose enough to show you are a lady.

    C. Do not accent any other part of your body in your dress other than your countenance. Doing so would be immodest.

    D. Wear extended or padded shoulders.

    E. Don't dress too trendy.

    F. Wear feminine dresses and classy suits, other than for truly casual events.

G. At an appropriate age, wear modest makeup. Do not wear too much makeup, but by the time a girl is an appropriate age, most men do prefer that she wear some makeup.

H. Keep your clothing neat and pressed.

I. Have manicured fingernails.

J. Watch your weight. Mothers do their daughters a great disservice when they do not teach them how to eat nutritionally. I believe in eating. God made us to eat in order to survive. I believe in eating four times a day and in eating all of the following at each meal: protein, fat, carbohydrates, and vegetables.

I keep my weight down by eating real food. I avoid all chemicals such as white flour, sugar, artificial sweeteners, preservatives, and so forth. I only eat whole grain real food. I avoid manmade, chemically processed food. If we teach our daughters to follow these principles and to eat moderate portions, we do them a great favor. We also do them a favor by teaching them moderate (not overly strenuous) exercise and by exercising with them.

K. Do not wear blue-jean skirts, sweatshirts, bobby socks, and tennis shoes too often. A girl can look cute to a man in casual clothes, but she should not be sloppy. Nor should she understate herself by wearing casual clothes all the time or where it is inappropriate.

All of these ideas about women's dress came from men. The idea is not necessarily to follow all of the abovementioned principles about dress. Rather, it is to teach your daughter to value the opinions of her father and to learn about dress mainly from him. Teach your daughter to please her father first in her dress, herself secondly, and other girls last. Most ladies' priorities of dress are just the opposite.

Bible Words to Teach
Your Daughter About Dress

- **Adorn** refers to "the well-designed plan of the universe." Your daughter's dress should be orderly and neat. *"Likewise, ye wives, be in subjection to your own husbands; that, if any obey not the word, they also may without the word be won by the conversation of the wives; While they behold your chaste conversation coupled with fear. Whose **adorning** let it not be that outward **adorning** of plaiting the hair, and of wearing of gold, or of putting on of apparel; But let it be the hidden man of the heart, in that which is not corruptible, even the ornament of a meek and quiet spirit, which is in the sight of God of great price. For after this manner in the old time the holy women also, who trusted in God, **adorned** themselves, being in subjection unto their own husbands."* (I Peter 3:1-5)

*"In like manner also, that women **adorn** themselves in modest apparel, with shamefacedness and sobriety; not with broided hair, or gold, or pearls, or costly array."* (I Timothy 2:9)

- **Modesty** means "balance or harmony." (I Timothy 2:9)
  Avoid wild hairstyles.
  Avoid clothes that are out of style.
  Avoid tight-fitting or short clothes.
  Avoid ill-fitting or dirty clothes.
- **Apparel** means "a let down or a flowing garment." (I Timothy 2:9)
- **Shamefacedness** means "quick to blush." Your daughter should be ashamed at the thought of her dress causing a man to think an unholy thought about her.
- **Sobriety** means "self-control." Teach your daughter to have self-control by thinking before she buys something. She should not buy something just because it is in style.
- **The attire of an harlot** is addressed in Proverbs 7:10 which says, *"And, behold, there met him a woman with the attire of an harlot, and subtil of heart."* There is an attire of an harlot. We should be sure our daughters are not wearing such clothing. A long skirt with a high slit was one of the signs of a harlot in Bible days.

- **Silk and purple** clothing was worn by the virtuous woman. *"She maketh herself coverings of tapestry; her clothing is silk and purple."* (Proverbs 31:22) Teach your daughter that a modest lady can be beautiful in her dress. She does not have to choose drab colors, nor does she have to choose practical fabrics.

Deuteronomy 22:5 teaches that it is an abomination to God for a woman to wear clothing which pertains to a man. *"The woman shall not wear that which pertaineth unto a man, neither shall a man put on a woman's garment: for all that do so are abomination unto the LORD thy God."* Though this advice is from the Old Testament, the words *"abomination to God"* must be noted. All laws that are an abomination to God do not change. The Bible teaches how unchanging our God is. For this reason, I taught my daughter not to wear trousers.

In 2006 newspaper headlines addressed the issue of a boy who was expelled from school because he wore an evening gown to a prom. A girl could have worn a tuxedo, and nothing would have been done. If most of my readers saw a man wearing a dress, they would probably think he was a pervert. Those same people can see their own daughter wearing trousers and say, "That is not clothing which pertains to a man." To this I say, "Selah" which means "think about it."

CONCLUSION

God truly did intend for boys and girls to be completely different, and **different is good!** But that difference is best cultivated through a heart that desires to be a help and a help meet. A young girl can best learn this principle by observing it in her own mother.

4

REARING
MASCULINE SONS

At this writing, a term that has suddenly become popular in American society is the term "metrosexual." I for one hate this term. It is a term used to describe a "city boy," or my dad might say a "pretty boy." A metrosexual is a man who gets a manicure or a pedicure, who styles his hair rather than cuts and combs it. It describes a man who is neither ruggedly masculine nor decidedly feminine.

"So God created man in his own image, in the image of God created he him; male and female created he them." (Genesis 1:27) It sounds to me like God wanted to put the genders on either one side or the other. He did not create a blended neutral gender in between. I do not claim to be the expert in rearing sons, but I did have two major goals in mind when I began to rear our son Kenny.

• I wanted to rear a son to serve the Lord—to do God's will.
• I wanted to rear a son who was very masculine.

Allow me to share some ideas about how **not** to rear a metrosexual.

1. From the earliest stages of life, don't dress your son in feminine or neutral clothes. I must admit that when Ken was a newborn baby, I did not start right away dressing him in blue jeans and Chicago Bears sweatshirts. He teases me about the pictures he sees of himself in his first Easter outfit—yellow overalls over a yellow and blue-striped shirt. As a tiny baby, Kenny had some outfits that were not rugged-looking. However, when Kenny began to walk, I quit dressing him in clothes that were not rugged-looking. His clothes may have been childish, but they were always definitely boyish. After hearing Kenny's opinion, I believe I would dress him in more boyish styles even earlier if I had it to do over again.

When Kenny was four years old, I tried to buy him a multi-colored winter coat. It had one or two small squares of hot pink and a couple of purple squares on it. "PINK AND PURPLE ARE GIRLS' COLORS," he proclaimed. "I WILL NOT WEAR THAT COAT."

Was I angered by his "putting his four-year-old foot down with his mother?" Perhaps I should have been, but I wasn't. I had two thoughts. First of all, I had a four-year-old son with masculine taste. Secondly, I reminded myself that a mother should not dress her son according to her own female tastes.

2. **Have your son play with masculine toys.** When our daughter was a baby, she slept each night with either a stuffed animal or a doll. When our son was just a toddler, he preferred sleeping with a hard metal truck or a golf ball. Kenny is particularly proud of his early taste for golf balls. This is an affinity that has stayed with him.

I do believe that a child is predisposed to like toys that are generally enjoyed by his or her gender. I also believe that a parent can have a great influence on a child by the kind of toys the parent encourages his child to play with.

3. **Teach the child to be physically coordinated.** I began when Kenny was a little boy playing every kind of Nerf sport there was. We often played Nerf baseball in our living room, not because I enjoyed trashing the living room unnecessarily, but because in the winter months, it was the only place we could play. Our sports moved outside in the summer. My husband played most of the sports with our son. Yet, because a mother is with her son so much of the time when he is young, I think that it is important that a mother not be a sissy in her approach to playing with her son.

I believe sports are important for teaching masculinity and character to a boy. However, sports are not life and death. Sports can bring out the worst in parents, so I believe it is important for parents such as myself to remind ourselves of this frequently.

4.   Teach your son to work. My dad advised me when I was rearing our children to leave the teaching of the Bible to my husband. Dad advised me to teach our children to work. My daughter, son, and I did many of the household chores together when our children were small. As I have already mentioned, when Kenny turned 12, he became the head caretaker of our property. When my husband became pastor and Kenny began working, we hired a lawn care service, but we still left Kenny in charge of many of the outdoor chores.

One of the things I admired about the father of my children is that he taught our son how to do many handyman jobs. My husband is literally a "Jack-of-all-trades." Every time he would fix a pipe under the sink or do any kind of fix-it job, he involved Kenny. From the age of four (maybe sooner) Kenny was involved in every job, all the way from the trip to the hardware store to the completion of the project.

5.   Do not allow your son to spend too much time alone. Both my husband and my father have had some experience in counseling homosexuals. Through my dad's counseling experience, he discovered that many immoral acts are begun when a boy is left to spend too much time alone. Even through Kenny's high school years, my husband and I spent a lot of time with him.

If just Jaclynn and I were going somewhere, we invited Kenny. If he said, as young adolescents are prone to do, "Aww, Mom, I don't want to go," I would say, "I want you to go; we'll make it fun." He almost always went, and we did have fun!

6.   Teach your daughter to help her brother become a man. When our children were still young, I taught Jaclynn that she was a part of helping her brother turn out right as a man. I explained that she could not boss her brother but must treat him with respect if she wanted him to learn to become a man.

I am grateful for a daughter who took my advice to heart. Until Kenny was married, if my husband and I were out of town, my daughter and son-in-law often planned something with our son without our asking them. A happy family is a team effort. Todd, Jaclynn, and Kenny have been there for each other during the death of my father, the transition of my husband to becoming pastor, and my receiving new duties as a pastor's wife. We could not have made it successfully without each member of our team.

7. **Do not allow your son to become off-balance in his love for music.** I do believe the Bible teaches that a man can be a musician. I think that rock music is simply an avenue whereby teenagers can express the many emotions that they feel. Teaching a young person to express his emotions through Christ-filled music is a great way to prevent his need or desire for rock music. The male musicians in our church are very masculine. I am thinking now of one outstanding musician in our ministries who is also a fiery preacher.

My father has said he never counseled a homosexual who did not have a love for classical music. The more a boy loves music, however, the more he needs his parents to keep that love in the proper focus in his life. If I had a boy who tended to be more studious than rugged, I do not think I would encourage him much in the area of music. This kind of boy definitely does not need a perfectionist mother demanding he stay at the piano bench for hours a day.

8. **Identify your son with his father.** Though our family was a team, we were also divided into two groups: the men and the girls. For example, the men ran to the hardware store while the girls put supper on the table. The men fixed the plumbing while the girls did the dishes. The men ate first, and the girls served them. It was not that one was better than the other. Each one of us enjoyed the role that God chose for us. We enjoyed our separate roles, we enjoyed being together, and we enjoyed teasing each other just a bit. "The men are the best!"; "No, the girls are the best!" and so forth. Even the teasing had its purpose—it was a fun way to stress gender identification.

From the time Kenny was a toddler, I knew that I did not rate compared to Dad. I was thrilled with that discovery—for I knew that my son had taken a step toward becoming a man. I wanted both of our children to favor Dad over me—but I knew this was important for my son in a unique way.

9. **Develop independence in your son.** When Kenny was 12 years old, I learned an amazing lesson. Men do not like to be told what

to do by a woman! From that time on, as much as possible, I avoided telling our son what to do. This was a challenge because Kenny's dad traveled a lot during Kenny's teen years. If I said, "You can't watch that on television," and Kenny argued, I would respond, "I'm sorry Kenny, but this is the rule Dad made. If you call Dad on the phone and he tells you otherwise, you may watch it. It's up to Dad."

This reply usually quieted Kenny. He did not like to argue with his plumbing buddy. He might disagree with a member of the other side—the girls' side, but it was hard to disagree with a fellow member of the men's team. This is not to say Kenny and I did not respect each other. To the contrary, it seemed that the more I pointed Kenny to his father, the more he respected me.

I know of some mothers who run along behind their sons barking orders left and right. They expect their sons to have perfect rooms, perfectly coiffed hair, etc. A house where there is a son will not be in perfect order. It does not have to be chaos; it can be lovely, but it will not be perfect.

10. Pay the price, but don't sacrifice obedience. My father advised my husband and me to expect strict obedience from our daughter—that is obedience with a sweet spirit. From Kenny, Dad advised that we expect complete obedience, but if he grumbled about his mom's telling him what to do, he advised that we overlook it. Just expect him to obey.

In closing, let me say that there is sacrifice to be made in rearing a man. A mother who is overly concerned about her reputation with other women may have a hard time with it. The house cannot always look like a page out of a *Better Homes and Gardens* magazine. Everything cannot be picture perfect where a man is being reared. Though others may scoff at such an idea, go ahead and make the sacrifices.

As I headed toward the empty nest and our son was living in the dormitories of Hyles-Anderson College, I must admit that the house almost never became disorderly when he was gone; the laundry hampers stayed almost empty through the week; nobody tracked muddy work boots or left tennis shoes on the floor. The house was awfully quiet sometimes, but even in its quiet, the walls seemed to ring with memories—not of yelling and screaming over spilled milk but of laughter shared among a happy family—the men and the girls—us four and no more—a team. And it's never long before one of our team members heads back in for a visit.

Am I thrilled that my house is immaculate? Someone even recently told me it looked like a house in *Better Homes and Gardens*! After several years of experience, I can tell you my two greatest thrills:

1. To have a husband who is used of God
2. To rear a child—to rear a man—who serves the Lord

May we all strive and pray together for both of these to be a reality in the lives of all of the families of fundamentalism.

5

THE KEY TO REARING
KINGS AND QUEENS

Proverbs 23:26, *"My son, give me thine heart, and let thine eyes observe my ways."* I just traded in my former vehicle for a bright red 2006 Mercury Mountaineer. Though I really love my new "set of wheels," I have one problem with it: it makes me obey. Yes, it is true—my SUV will not do a thing I say until I first do what it says. It demands that I put the right key in the ignition. It will not respond to a house key, to an office key, or to a Chevy key; I have to use the right key. I can yell at my vehicle and say, "You better obey me first. If it wasn't for me, you wouldn't even be in this garage," but it does me no good.

My Mountaineer still makes it first command: "Find the right key, put it in my ignition, and turn it. Then, and only then, will I do whatever you tell me to do."

So it is with child rearing. Yes, I did bring my children into the world. If it weren't for me, they wouldn't even be here. But the responsibility falls upon me first to find the right key to our children's heart and to use it to win their hearts. When I have won their heart, then and only then can I expect them to *"observe my ways"*—to follow my example and to obey me.

Jesus continually does things to win our hearts. The Bible says, *"For the LORD's portion is his people."* (Deuteronomy 32:9a) *Portion* means "all He wants." All the Lord wants is His people. The birds, the flowers, the trees, and all of nature are simply used to draw us to God. So many times I ask God to answer silly prayers, and He does it. Why? He wants to win my heart to Him. I love to see hummingbirds. I often ask God to show them to me, and He sends them at the strangest places. He does this, not because He has nothing better to do, but rather because He is the Master at finding the right key to reach His children's hearts.

He shouldn't have to do this. After all, if it weren't for God, I would not be here. He's already done enough, after all. Just think of Calvary! But He continues to send hummingbirds and to answer seemingly insignificant prayers. God cares enough to relate with my human desires and to care about the minute details of my life.

If we love our children, we must find a key that is appropriate to them and use it continually to win their hearts.

1. Care enough to find the right key. Parents need to elevate the job of child rearing. So many mothers are tossing the job of child rearing into the laps of day-care workers while they pursue the seemingly more important tasks in the career world. They are so exhausted by the time they get home from work, they barely have enough strength to cook supper and get the children in bed, much less finding a key to reach their hearts.

Several years ago the diamond fell out of my engagement ring. This was a ring I had been wearing for over 20 years. I was only without the diamond for 45 minutes. I was fortunate enough to find the diamond glistening in the carpet on my side of the bed. How happy I was when I found the diamond again.

A story in the Bible relates how a woman searched until she found one valuable coin that she had lost. The Bible describes her great rejoicing at finding that coin. God uses this story as a parable to illustrate the great care He takes to win just one soul to Himself. We should copy the example of our heavenly parent and go to great lengths to win our children's heart to us.

The heart cry of King David in II Samuel 18:33 is *"O my son Absalom, my son, my son Absalom! would God I had died for thee, O Absalom, my son, my son!"* Absalom was a rebel whom David could not bring himself to deal with. Absalom's rebellion caused him to try to overthrow his father's kingdom. Yet when it was too late, David realized what a great loss it was to have to part with even the most rebellious of sons. Sometimes we don't realize how important things are until it is too late.

2. Use a different key for each child. You would not want to use the same key for a boy that you would for a girl. A small child will require a completely different key than a teenager. Likewise, each individual will need a different key according to his individual personality. A parent must spend a lot of time with each child individually so that he will know each of them well enough to find their key. I tried in each stage of our children's lives not to let 24 hours pass without doing something fun with them on an individual basis. I took a mini-vacation with our children every day.

3. Use a different key for each age. The following are some ideas of keys I used with my children. This is not an exhaustive list of all that I did, but they are examples to give you ideas. Remember, "Ideas beget ideas, and excuses beget excuses."

A. Keys I Used for Babies. Some keys I used for babies included singing, rocking, holding, and cuddling.

B. Keys I Used for Small Children. I participated in reading, playing school, playing with dolls, taking walks, swinging, biking, playing Nerf sports in the house, playing board games, catching fireflies, baking, gardening, and picking flowers with my children.

C. Keys I Used for Rearing Teenagers. I quit traveling and speaking. I attended their activities. I loved their friends. I made them feel mature and needed. I made my son feel masculine. I took them shopping. I sang with them at the piano. I asked for their advice. I approached chores gently through the use of notes or questions. I played tennis, roller bladed, golfed, and went miniature golfing. I shot fireworks with them. I went sledding and hiking with them. I took our daughter to pick fruits and vegetables. I went go-karting with them.

I remember going on a mini-vacation with Kenny one day when he was about four and finding a toad. I had always hated toads until then. But when I saw Kenny with the toad, suddenly the toad looked beautiful. The toad was a key to my four-year-old's heart. Kenny and I caught the toad and put him a jar with holes in the lid. Just after catching the toad, Kenny and I took a nap in my queen-sized bed.

I had told Kenny that since I loved him so much, I would let him pick up the toad and put it in the jar. The truth was I was afraid to pick up the toad, but I didn't want Kenny to know it. That could cause some serious loss of a little boy's heart.

"Mom," said Kenny, "because I love you so much, you can put Toby [the name of our toad] on the night stand beside you as you sleep." I'll never forget the nerve-wracking time of rest I had with the toad trying to escape from that jar while I was trying to get some sleep!

4. If you can't find a key, get help. Other than my husband, I used my pastor-father to help me when I was puzzled about how to reach the hearts of our children. I remember two times in particular when he gave me a key to helping our children. Once was when Jaclynn was two, and the other time was when Kenny was about twelve.

5. Don't throw away a key for no good reason. I believe a lot of good parents lose their children when they are teenagers because they do not choose carefully what battles they are willing to fight with their children. One key for rearing teenagers can be their friends. Both of my children had wonderful friends. But I did not always approve 100 percent of all of our children's friends. Instead of fighting my children on this matter and demanding that all of their friends be as perfect as them (in my own biased opinion), I spent a lot of time with their friends and became a friend to them. I almost never criticized our children's friends, and I frequently bragged on them.

It was not our first desire for our children to date in high school. When Jaclynn was a junior in high school, her friends had boyfriends. When Jaclynn became interested in a fine young man, we allowed her to befriend him. Our entire family befriended him. They eventually went their separate ways, but I do believe God gave us wisdom not to force our daughter to be different than her peers in this situation. What could have become a wall between us became a bridge and a key to our daughter's heart.

I am not saying that a parent should never put his foot down with his teenager, but I am saying one should choose his battles carefully. There are enough battles that must be fought with teenagers, so it is important to only fight the really necessary ones. Sometimes parents create battles because they are striving for their child to meet their pre-conceived ideas or their perfectionist standards. Parents also like to fight unnecessary battles in order to separate children from their peers in order to make their children seem superior to their peers. All of this is unwise.

6

WHY DON'T WE FIND THE RIGHT KEY?

1. We are too busy. I was riding with Kenny when he was a teenager, and he brought up the fact that he remembered playing a lot with me when he was a child. We played every kind of sport there was. We played baseball in the side yard during the summer and every kind of Nerf sport you can imagine in the winter. I was surprised that Kenny brought up this subject. "I'm surprised you remember," I stated.

"I remember," he replied.

I sometimes questioned myself when I was rearing our children. I was having so much fun with them that I felt downright slothful. I read a definition of the word *slothful* that really helped me. Slothfulness is using your time in any way other than the way God wants you to use it. Though I sometimes stood on a baseball field thinking, "For this I got a college degree?" I knew I was using my time the way God wanted me to use it.

One morning in my devotions, after having questioned myself the day previously, I read Psalm 37:7 which says, *"Rest in the LORD, and wait patiently for him: fret not thyself because of him who prospereth in his way...."* I had many friends who were already very successful in some area of career or ministry. I felt that life was passing me by. God used this verse to reassure me that I was doing right.

Now our children are grown and married. Compared to his preschool days, I rarely see our son. I am happy, however, because Kenny has a wonderful wife and he is serving the Lord. I am even more comforted by the fact that I enjoyed Kenny every second that he lived in our home, as I did Jaclynn. I cannot think of anything a mother could do with her children that I did not do with mine. Now I am availing myself of opportunities I once denied myself. God has truly blessed this stage of my life in great and mighty ways that I knew not.

I have found that opportunities come, go and usually come back again, especially if they are rejected for the right reason. However, stages of relationships do not. Once a stage is past, it is gone forever.

I am comforted by Kenny's words that he spoke to me in high school, "I remember."

2. **We are too angry.** King David was angry with his son Absalom. Absalom had murdered his brother because his brother had raped Absalom's sister Tamar. Absalom went away, and David did not seek his return until he was compelled to by Joab.

At the request of Joab, David allowed Absalom's return to the kingdom, but he never restored his relationship with his son.

I often see this type of response by parents of teenage and adult children. The child does something that angers his parent, and that parent refuses to continue to build a relationship with the child.

3. **We are too proud.** We often know what the key is for building a relationship; we are just too proud to use it. The key to building a broken relationship is usually found in that thing that irritates you. Are you irritated about your friend's new house? The new house is the key to building a relationship with your friend. Does your friend brag incessantly until you are tempted to throw away that friendship? Use the key of bragging to build that relationship.

4. **We just don't care enough to fix the relationship.** It is easy to love a cute little toddler when he hurts you. But a big, awkward teenager is not as easy to love, especially when he doesn't love you back. One of the reasons we as parents do not love our teenagers as we should is that we have not developed our own love past a teenage-type of love. We only love what pleases us and what causes love to come naturally.

Matthew 5:48 says, *"Be ye therefore perfect, even as your Father which is in heaven is perfect."* This admonition comes after several verses where God is teaching about love, particularly about loving your enemies. This Bible word *perfect* means "mature." We are to be mature in our love according to God's commands. Mature love is loving the unlovable. A parent should care enough to find the right key for loving his child, even when his child seems unlovable.

THE UNIVERSAL KEY
There is a universal key for loving your child.

PRAYER + PRAISE + ACTION =
A DEVELOPED PARENT/CHILD RELATIONSHIP.

1. **Prayer.** A mother should pray daily and several hours a week for her child. She should pray about every area of his life. If she is awakened in the night, she should get up and go to the child's doorway, fall on her knees and pray for her child to turn out right and for God to help her find the right key for her child. In Luke 11:5-13, God uses a parable to teach us the importance of praying at midnight. A mother should fast for her child. I have done several 24 hours fasts, not letting anyone know at the time, while I prayed especially for several specific needs, including my children.

2. **Praise.** Proverbs 27:21 says, *"As the fining pot for silver, and the furnace for gold; so is a man to his praise."* Praise paints a picture for your child of what he could become, and he will begin to act out that picture.

Find your child's weakness and use the tool of praise to help your child in that area. Suppose you have a shy child. Don't criticize your child for being shy. CRITICISM AND NAGGING LOCK THE DOOR. PRAISE IS THE KEY THAT OPENS IT. Praise the child's ability with people; praise his personality; praise his sense of humor. Every time you see that child acting the opposite of his weakness, praise that child. Teach a shy child to smile by telling him how beautiful his smile is.

3. **Action.** Spending time with your child is part of the action that will build your child. Also, setting a good example in their area of weakness is a great key for building children. For example, you can teach a

shy child to smile by regularly giving away smiles yourself.

Shyness is just one weakness that can be solved by the key of PRAYER + PRAISE + ACTION. You can fill in the blank with any weakness and use the same equation to bring the same positive result. By the way, this equation is also the key for a wife's completing a husband in marriage.

OTHER KEYS FOR REARING CHILDREN

1. Accept your child. Ask God to make your child what God wants him to be, not what you want him to be. Don't expect your child to be perfect.

2. Don't manipulate your child to meet your needs. When our daughter started college, she moved into the dormitories. Jaclynn attended our own Bible college, affiliated with our church, so she only moved 15 minutes from home. I am almost embarrassed to say how much I missed her; I cried for four weeks.

I had so enjoyed Jaclynn's senior year of high school. I had done my part to see it was one of the best years of her life. I had done a lot of chaperoning and attended most of my daughter's senior activities.

It seemed strange to give so much of your life to a person and then to feel her pried from your hands. That is the way it felt to me.

College was different. I almost never saw Jaclynn. She came home on the weekends but was gone all weekend working on her bus route at church. The reality that I was not rearing Jaclynn for my own fulfillment set in, and it set in hard. I read the love chapter (I Corinthians 13) a lot, and I remembered the verse II Corinthians 12: 15, *"And I will very gladly spend and be spent for you; though the more abundantly I love you, the less I be loved."*

I accepted the fact that I was to be there for Jaclynn only when she needed me and not when I needed her. I also accepted the fact that Christ is all I need.

Then I set about to find a new key for this new stage of life.

- I made treats for her and her roommates.
- I sent her cards at the college.
- I took her friends to Walmart and out to eat.

- I gave her roommates rides home from church, and we all stopped for ice cream.
- I chaperoned groups to outings in Chicago.

I comforted myself by remembering all of the ways I had savored each stage of Jaclynn's life. I joined the adult choir at church. This is something I had always wanted to do but put off to sit with our children in church. I had no regrets.

One of the saddest verses in the Bible is the verse where King David laments the death of his son Absalom. II Samuel 18:33 says, *"And the king was much moved, and went up to the chamber over the gate, and wept: and as he went, thus he said, O my son Absalom, my son, my son Absalom! would God I had died for thee, O Absalom, my son, my son!"* Just a few days after Absalom's death the Bible says in II Samuel 19:14 that David *"...bowed the heart of all the men of Judah, even as the heart of one man...."*

David was good with people. He knew the keys to getting people to follow him, but he failed to win the heart of his own son. David did not seem to realize the tragedy of his mistake until it was too late. Then he wished to die rather than to live without the son he had so long neglected. May we learn from King David's mistake and care enough to find the right key for our children.

Mark 9:36, 37, *"And he took a child, and set him in the midst of them: and when he had taken him in his arms, he said unto them, Whosoever shall receive one of such children in my name, receiveth me: and whosoever shall receive me, receiveth not me, but him that sent me."*

Mark 9:42, *"And whosoever shall offend one of these little ones that believe in me, it is better for him that a millstone were hanged about his neck, and he were cast into the sea."*

Mark 10:14, *"But when Jesus saw it, he was much displeased, and said unto them, Suffer the little children to come unto me, and forbid them not: for of such is the kingdom of God."*

7

COMMON MISTAKES PARENTS MAKE IN CHILD REARING

My friend, Cathy Kimmel, once asked me how I got so much wisdom to know what to do in rearing our children. I told Cathy that a lot of my "wisdom" came from trial and error. I made a lot of mistakes in my child rearing, but it is usually not the mistakes that I share with others. Again, let me remind our readers that only the grace and mercy of God rears good children, and only God should get the credit for any successes. Let me also mention that my mom and dad were my chief child-rearing counselors. I don't think God minds my giving them some of the credit, also.

I really enjoyed having children; to me, rearing them was just plain fun. I tried to find as many ways as I could to teach Jaclynn and Kenny, not so I could write it in a book someday, but so I could give my best to my child-rearing years.

Let me share some of the common mistakes of child rearing with you.

1.   **Parents have no vision for their child.** Proverbs 29:18, *"Where there is no vision, the people perish: but he that keepeth the law, happy is he."* In any relationship where there is no vision, the relationship is on a downhill slide. Many a couple lives life with a vision of obtaining material things; once they have obtained their executive house, two luxury

cars, and had their 2.5 children (the American average), the marriage begins to suffer.

So it is with child rearing. A mother/child relationship without a vision will consist mainly of a lot of complaining by the mother about muddy footprints on the floor, messy hand prints on the wall, and so forth.

Our son Kenny is 6 foot 2 inches and around 190 pounds. We live in a relatively small, quaint country home. When Kenny lived at home, I often teased him about being a bull in a china shop. Without a vision, Kenny's knocking something over was a pain in the neck. With a vision, however, Kenny's presence in our home was an honor worth any clean-up that may have needed to be done.

When Kenny was born, we gave him three names: his given name is Kenneth Jack Frasure Schaap. His first name is after my husband's father whom we admire very much. His second name is after my husband and my father. His third name is really after my Grandma Hyles who passed away two months before Kenny was born. I was very close to this godly lady, and it grieves me that Kenny never met her.

There is one other reason that I gave Kenny three names; it is that Princess Diana did the same. I felt that if Princess Diana felt her sons were royal enough to receive an extra name, so was mine. I desired, after all, to rear a prince with God. The extra name, I felt, would be a good reminder of this. I feel the same way about Kenny's wife Candace.

I also feel the same way about our daughter Jaclynn and our son-in-law Todd. I pray daily that God will use them in "great and mighty ways which I know not." It is a privilege to have a part in each of our children's lives.

2. Parents have too much vision for their child. Though I believe in having a vision for a child, I do not believe in dreaming specifically about what a child might do. I do not spend my time daydreaming about my son's being a prince with the world or a prince in fundamental circles. I pray for him to be a prince with God. I want our children to fulfill God's purpose for their life. That purpose may be one that brings them position and authority, or it may be one that is unknown, except by God. My son may become a great man of God, or he may become a great encourager of a great man of God. I only want him to fulfill the purpose which God has for him and his wife Candace.

I have reminded my son often that there is nothing he must do to make his dad and me proud of him. We are already proud that Kenny is our son. Our desire is for Kenny to find and do whatever God's will is for him. I feel the same way about Jaclynn and Todd. We are already overjoyed at their accomplishments; we expect nothing more.

A mother who believes otherwise may become pushy. She may expect her son to achieve great things for God. Good may not be good enough. This will discourage a child, because it is a parent's acceptance and approval that is most motivating to a child who is seeking to serve the Lord.

A mother who believes otherwise may become competitive with other parents, thereby failing to teach her child how to properly relate with others. I don't just want my children to become a prince or a princess with God; I want others' children to become this, too.

Also, a mother who believes otherwise may push her child toward some secular job promising financial success rather than praying that her child will find and do the will of God.

Remember, we should not be living our lives through our children. We are not building our own little princes for our own kingdom; neither are we building princes for this world or for our fundamental peers. We are building princes for the Lord Jesus Christ! Tell your children you are proud of them! Say it boldly; say if often.

How pleased you and your child will be in eternity when our Saviour says, "You have finished your course!"

3. **Parents have too much concern for their own reputation.** When my children were small, I worked on not correcting them in public. My dad taught me that correcting children in public takes away a parent's need to train them in private.

When Jaclynn was in two-year-old Sunday school, the teacher gave her a cookie each week before she left. Each Sunday I stood in line and watched as mothers picked up their children. Most of the mothers reminded their child to say thank you to the teacher who gave them the cookie. I wanted to do the same thing, but I remembered my commitment to not correct my child publicly.

Many weeks after Jaclynn joined the two year olds, we played Sunday school during our training time. Jaclynn loved to pretend and enjoyed what she thought was just play. When our pretend Sunday school was dismissed, I (as the pretend teacher) gave Jaclynn a cookie and asked her to practice saying "Thank you."

Several weeks went by before Jaclynn remembered on her own to associate the Sunday school practice at home with real Sunday school. It seemed at times that she was the only one who was not saying "Thank you" for the cookie in Sunday school, and yes, I was embarrassed. But I was starting a precedent in my thinking and in my behavior that I'm glad I started. Here is some of what I was thinking.

"Jaclynn is not an object brought into this world to make me look good. She is not to be cajoled, pushed, pulled, and reprimanded for all the world to see. Jaclynn is a person with feelings who will grow to be a valuable adult. The best time to start treating her with respect is now. She is on loan to me to be trained at home. With proper training, she will learn to do right on her own without my help."

Jaclynn did eventually learn to say thank you on her own for her cookie in Sunday school, and I learned something even more valuable which would be needed more and more through the child-rearing years. I learned that my reputation was not the issue in my child rearing.

Through the years I have avoided, when at all possible, correcting my children or my teenagers publicly or even in front of one or two of their friends.

4. **Parents do not use enough positive methods in child rearing.** Several years ago I read an object lesson that helped me immensely as I was training our children. A child's heart should be compared to the gas tank in a car. As long as the tank is full of gas, we have a right to expect it to run properly. If the car is not running and it is full of gas, there is a problem that must be fixed. If, however, the car is empty of gas, we do not expect the car to function properly.

If I discover that my car is empty of gas, I become frustrated not with the car, but with myself. I do not kick the car and say, "You rebellious car, why don't you behave?" Instead, I remind myself of what I need to do to put the gas in the car before it runs out.

So it is with children. Much of children's misbehavior is caused by lack of attention. It is my responsibility to fill my child's heart with the following: praise, appropriate touch, time (for training and fun), and eye contact.

As long as my children were full of these, I had every right to expect them to behave properly. If they did not, I knew there was a problem that needed to be fixed, probably through a spanking. I felt confident when my decision to spank came because I knew their gas tanks were full.

I imagined in my mind's eye that my children's gas tank became empty through the night. Each morning they awoke with empty hearts that needed to be refilled as soon as possible with praise, appropriate touch, time, and eye contact. The home is the service station, and the parent is the service attendant who must be responsible for consistently filling the child's emotional tank.

Much of what psychiatrists are calling Attention Deficit Disorder (ADD) can probably be attributed to neglect of positive methods used by parents. Children are living their lives with empty hearts and unfilled emotional tanks. They are simply unable to function properly. How does the world solve this problem? They say, "Drug the child so he won't be a problem to the parent." The child is sedated, and the neglect is continued. The child now not only has an empty heart but also a dull mind damaged by the effects of unnecessary drugs. I understand that there may be a time to use drugs with your children, and I am not trying to judge individual situations, but I have no doubt that drugs are overused in our country, especially in controlling the behavior of children.

Not long after I addressed the subject of ADD in *Christian Womanhood*, I received a copy of an article from *The Doctor's Prescription for Healthy Living* (Volume 7 Number 4). This article contained the following quote: "Ritalin is an amphetamine and works on the central nervous system, acting in a similar way to cocaine on the brains of children not suffering from ADHD." Once again let me reiterate that there may be a legitimate time for a child with a brain injury to use drugs. But again let me caution, sometimes these drugs are being prescribed unnecessarily. I recommend that they be avoided if at all possible.

I have included a poem that I wrote to our daughter Jaclynn and one that I wrote to our son Kenny. I rarely bragged on my children publicly when they were young. It is not always appropriate to brag excessively on our children, especially to those who have children the same age. I did, however, brag on our children daily to them, and I continue to do so to this day. The following poems are not to show what great children I have reared, though they are great ones, but to show you how I feel and how I express my feelings to my children. I want these poems to show ways in which I want you to make your children feel that you care about them.

You're an Angel to Me

Before you were born, I saw you in a dream
Awake I did think; in my mind it did seem
She's an angel to me!

Then you came along; I saw you with my eyes.
Your dad looked with me, and we saw
    quite a prize.
You're an angel to us!

Sweet baby you were, with a smile sweet and wide.
You brought us such joy, and you rarely did cry.
You're an angel to me!

As our little girl, you were thoughtful and sweet.
Your dad and I felt that you couldn't be beat.
You're an angel to us!

Your cute brother came; he was born with two moms.
You bossed him a bit and held him in your arms.
You're an angel to me!

As a teen, you loved all and reached out to the sad.
We saw 'twas an angel in our home we had.
You're an angel to us!

You prayed on your knees, looked to God with a smile.
I knew in my heart this was no normal child.
You're an angel to me!

Dear God, I would ask, "Was I good in this world?
You sent me an angel instead of a girl."
You're an angel to me!

Perhaps I was such a bad mom I'm afraid.
God chose to send me a young lady premade.
You're an angel to me.

I know you get busy; your things you can't find.
It's hard to get mad at an angel so kind.
You're an angel to me!

With eye-crinkled smile and so much curly hair,
Sometimes you may seem an angel unaware.
You're an angel to me!

Be patient, my sweet, with your parents this year.
It's hard to let go of an angel so dear.
You're an angel to us!

You'll fly from our nest, straight and quickly you'll fly.
An angel you'll be to some real lucky guy.
You're an angel to me!

You'll follow him well; God will have quite a plan
For an angel so sweet and her own special man.
You're an angel to me!

Your life may seem simple; your life may seem grand.
You may live next door or away 'cross the land.
Whatever you do or wherever you'll be,
I'll be somewhere saying, "You're an angel to me!"

TO MY SON KENNY
(3-20-2000)

When you were born, I'd pray that God would
    give to me a son.
It's hard for me to tell just now how much I
    wanted one.
I told the Lord the son He'd lend I'd give back
    right away.
I would not use this son for self or getting my
    own way.

And when the doctor looked at me and said that it's a boy,
I wept; I cried; I thanked the Lord, and shouted with great joy.
Then told the Lord this son He'd lent, I'd give back right away;
I would not use this son for self or getting my own way.

I brought a precious baby home. Your dad, along with me,
Would stare and gaze upon your face and promise happily.
We'd tell the Lord this son He'd lent, so sweet in every way,
Would not be ours, but would be His to use in any way.

You grew to be a little boy, the "funnest" sort of kind.
I laughed and played each day with you, not wasting any time.
For in my heart, I knew the time would come when you'd be gone.
I knew that you were really not a gift, but just a loan.

Now you're a man of younger sort, so handsome and so tall.
I see my son and know that God has sent the best of all.
I oft' remind myself that you're not really here to stay.
For long before the day you came, I'd given you away.

I know I've told this tale to you, perhaps too many times.
Yet now I feel I want this tale for you to be in rhyme.
I say once more that, when the doctor said you were a boy,
Dad wept; I cried; we thanked the Lord, and shouted with great joy.

There's nothing you must do in life to make us proud you're ours.
The first time that we saw you, we both knew you were a star.
We only ask you help us keep the promise we have made—
Just give your life to God, my son, and let Him have His way.

In closing this point, may I ask, "Does your child feel valuable to you?" Is his emotional tank full of praise, appropriate touch, time, and eye contact? Hopefully, the service station is open and the service attendants who read this chapter can quickly refill any empty tanks. Please do it today!

5. **Parents do not provide enough private time for their children.** In 1983 the Lord gave us a cute country home. When we moved into the house, I promised the Lord that I would use it for Him. We have hosted many parties in our home, especially in the summertime, because God gave us a beautiful large yard with our home. When my husband was the Sunday school teacher for the Singles Department of our church (the college and career class), we had yearly parties at our house. We have had over 100 at a time at a party.

We have hosted Blue Denim and Lace, our junior-age girls' club; the adult choir; and other groups in our house. But our home is not Grand Central Station. Most of the time, we have used our home as a private retreat for our family. Our home is located 30 minutes from our church. We live in a very small town, and our world completely changes when we enter our neighborhood. Our house looks more like it belongs in Mayberry than near Hammond, Indiana.

One of my favorite ways to use my home is to invite some lady who is struggling to sit with me in my living room (hopefully over a cup of coffee) and to encourage her. My time for this is limited, but I do enjoy this. However, I never counsel when my family is home, and our family does not encourage people to stop by unannounced.

As a former preacher's kid and as a pastor's wife, let me testify that a pastor's family really does feel a unique type of pressure. They are watched all of the time. Preachers' kids have a unique opportunity to glorify the Lord and their parents. On the other hand, if they have a bad day and their behavior brings some type of shame to Christ and their parents, the whole church will probably be watching. One of my favorite statements about home is this: Home is where the pressure comes off!

The amount of time spent entertaining in the home should be up to the tastes of your husband and children. When our married daughter Jaclynn lived at home, I sometimes thought she would prefer having guests all of the time. Brother Schaap and Kenny, however, are more private.

Soon after Jaclynn got married, we redesigned our basement and family room into a recreation room where Kenny could comfortably bring his friends. As the only child living at home, he was at a time in his life when he enjoyed bringing his guy friends over frequently. Kenny's friends were welcome when I was home, but I did not entertain friends when Kenny was home. Rarely do we have people over when my husband is home. This is his private time with the family.

6. **Parents do not have enough fun interaction with their children.** The well-known preacher, Dewitt Talmage, once said that home should be a place of cheerfulness and gaiety. I could not agree with him more. At our house, the pressure comes off, and the fun begins. In my own biased opinion, everyone in our family has a great sense of humor. You might call it a sick or a silly sense of humor, but I call it great (in my own biased opinion).

When our children were little, I tried not to let 24 hours pass without doing something fun with them that they enjoyed doing. I scheduled this activity into my day. When they became teens, I changed that to at least once a week. We now have a bi-weekly family night with our son and his wife and our daughter and her husband. Every other Tuesday evening, we eat dinner together and usually play games as a family together. At our house just downright silliness was and is allowed!

7. **Parents allow their children to watch too much television.** Television is a convenient baby sitter, but it grows worse all of the time in its content. What our children see and hear definitely does affect their behavior as well as their spiritual temperature.

When our children were very small, I allowed them to watch one television program a day. That program had to be pre-approved. As the television commercials got worse, we made a new rule. There would be no television watching without a parent in the room. We only allowed our children to watch pre-approved videos (one a day).

As our children got older, we moved the television out of the family room. (Our family room was set away from the rest of the house.) We put the television in a more central location so that the television could not take our children away from the family. I understand that this can cause the family to watch too much television, but for us this has worked. Television is not a real temptation for me. Typically, I watch a few minutes of the evening news from time to time, and that is all. All of our families' television watching is very limited. We may rarely watch a news show, but we do not watch any prime-time television sitcoms or adventure series.

We did not have Internet service or cable in our home when our children were living at home. My husband and I decided there was nothing good on the Internet or cable television that made it worth the bad that was at our children's disposal via these modes of communication. As television grows almost pornographic, the same decision might need to be made by the Christian families in America. You may disagree with Brother Schaap's and my philosophy about the Internet, but it is our years of counseling that have made us so leery of the Internet. If you must have the Internet, find a way to make it impossible for your children and teenagers to have access to it when they are alone.

I spent a lot of time with my children while they were growing up. I built my life around them, as well as around my husband. Someone once said to me, "You spend so much time with your children; you are going to fall apart when they grow up."

Quite the opposite is true! I feel great peace. I may see a mother somewhere enjoying her child in a way that I used to enjoy mine. My first reaction may be a tinge of sadness when I realize those days are over. My second quick reaction is always this: I enjoyed my child in that way when he/she was young. There is nothing we did not enjoy. Then a peace settles over me and tells me that I do not need to look back.

8. **Parents depend too much on the Christian school to rear their children.** Both of our children could read before they started kindergarten. At the time, I didn't go around telling people this; I was

not in competition with other's children. I just enjoyed playing school with our children, and I noticed that they loved to learn. The day they read their first words was a thrill of my life and one that I got to enjoy instead of their teacher. I was, however, concerned that their "over-preparation" for kindergarten would cause behavior problems when they did start school. My worries were unfounded.

As our children reached school age, I scheduled time each evening to help them with their homework. I enjoyed these moments together. I realize that families with multiple children and slow learners will face greater hardships in the area of homework. I am not for pushing your child beyond his capabilities; I am simply for doing your best with each child. The point is that school to me was never a replacement for the people who should be their children's primary teachers—their parents.

9. **Parents do not require their children to do enough work.** If a parent cannot get his child to work, perhaps the problem is that he has not worked enough with his child. I loved working with my children. When they were preschool age, I taught them to do simple chores like folding washcloths and small pieces of laundry.

My favorite chore with my children was planting flowers. When flower planting time came, I put the tape recorder on the deck and turned on Patch the Pirate tapes. (As a mother of young adults, I am starting to miss Patch the Pirate!) With our cheerful music around us, we (Jaclynn, Ken, and I) planted around 100 annuals each year. (Hooray for my husband who has financed my love for flowers! When the salesman at the nursery asks me what kind of flowers I want, I say "Yes.")

What fun I had working with our children. These are precious memories. I hope somewhere along the way, they got the idea that work is truly fun!

10. **Parents allow their children to have too much idle time and/or too much time with their peers.** When our children were small and all through most of their school years, I took them to school as opposed to having them ride a bus or in a carpool. I know that either of these can be necessary, but both can provide the child with unnecessary idle time and time with peers.

Most of our rides to and from school were fun. (Okay, I'll admit we had a few late mornings and bad hair days when the ride to school was less than fun.) We sometimes left early and stopped for breakfast. On one of the first nice spring mornings each year, we ate breakfast at McDonald's in the car with all of the windows rolled down. Each day as I drove to pick up my children from school, I yielded myself anew to the Holy Spirit and asked Him to help me as I spent time with Jaclynn and Kenny. We sometimes stopped for ice cream on the way home, and most of all, we enjoyed talking to each other.

The following are some other ways we prevented our children from having too much time with peers or idle time:

A. We did not allow our children to attend slumber parties.
B. We rarely allowed our children to spend the night at someone else's house.
C. We rarely left our children with baby sitters. If we did, it was usually for my soul-winning time or for my weekly date with my husband.
D. We chose baby sitters who spent time with our children. I am indebted to people like Sandy Moore and Arischa Akin who made baby-sitting our children more like a ministry than a job.
E. When our children could drive, we asked them to come straight home from school unless there was a planned church or school activity. When they did go somewhere, we asked questions like,
   - "Where are you going?"
   - "What time is it over? Come straight home."
   - "Will adults be there?"
   - "What adults will be there?"

Even when our children were teenagers, we did not allow them to go to a friend's house unless a parent would be home.

In our large ministry, I have had the opportunity to watch hundreds and perhaps thousands of teenagers grow up. Many of them have gone through a rebellious stage. I believe the key element that causes those to do something tragic during this stage is too much freedom. I know young adults who never recovered from the things they did during their rebellious stage. I also know young adults who are now serving the Lord who once hung around with those same people. Why? I believe it is because they were not given the same freedom as their friends were when they were in that rebellious stage.

11. **Parents do not promote clear leadership in the home.** I cannot tell you how important it is that one person be in charge in the family, that the person in charge is the father, and that it be distinctly clear that Dad is in charge.

Let me share some ideas of how to make this happen:

- Refer your children's questions to Dad when he is home, even small questions like, "Can I have a piece of candy?" Transfer of leadership should be evident when Dad comes home.
- Yield to Dad in conflict, such as setting the thermostat where Dad likes it. Think ahead and list what those conflicts might be.
- Ask Dad to make all of the little and big decisions in the house. Let Dad choose the exit on the expressway, even if it means getting lost. Let Dad choose the restaurant and plan the family activities. List small decisions that Dad can make.
- Wait hand and foot upon Dad.
- Be respectful in your body language and tone of voice toward Dad.
- Never criticize Dad.
- Honor Dad. Make a huge deal out of him!

I haven't always succeeded at these things, but I have tried them, and I feel that my husband, my children, and I all came out the winners for my having tried them.

12. **Parents do not have proper priorities in the home.** Marriage should come first, and children should come second. The following are some ideas on how to keep the marriage first in your home.

- Have a weekly date night for Mom and Dad to be alone.
- Never disagree on your spouse's discipline.

- Do not allow your children to sit between you in church or in the car and so forth.
- Allow your children to see you express appropriate affection to each other.

If God intends a child to be reared in a home where the marriage comes before the children, and I believe the Bible teaches that He does, then a child who is placed before his mother or father will turn out to be an emotionally or a spiritually warped child.

13. Parents do not show enough clear support for the authorities in their children's lives. My husband often says, "It takes a team to rear a child." A few times an authority in our children's lives seemed to be mistreating them. I think I can honestly say that 99 percent of the time I kept my mouth shut. I regret the few times that I did not, and I tried to catch myself so that I would not repeat my mistake.

Once my child made a critical statement about one of his authorities at school. I proceeded to tell that child about what that person had been through and all of the virtues of that person. Before I knew it, I began to cry. To be honest with you, I was embarrassed that I had allowed myself to become emotional about the whole situation. But looking back, I think I am glad that I did. To my knowledge, my child never said another unkind statement about that person in our home, and that child became very good friends with that authority. This person later became one of the chief influences during an important stage of my child's life. I wonder what would have happened if I had not handled that situation as I did.

I believe the most important part of child rearing is making Dad the hero or treating your husband the way you want your children to treat you, authority, and most of all, God. I believe following this one point could make the difference in your child rearing and in your marriage. Remember, your husband may only become as great as you treat him. Also, you will only respect your husband as much as you honor him. Try it; you'll like it. I tried it and have come out the winner every time!

14. Parents push children to grow up too soon. I believe that a prudent method of leading a child to wisdom and maturity is to allow that child plenty of time to be just that—a child. I have grown up in a large church which has allowed me to observe thousands of children as they grew up. In my observations, I have learned that boys in particular struggle more in their teen and early adult years if, for one reason or another, they grow up too soon. Allow me to give you some suggestions concerning this particular point.

A. *Give a child plenty of time to be close to his mother.* A child should be given plenty of rocking and cuddling when he/she is small. Small boys, especially, will not mature properly into manhood if they are not allowed to be tender and sweet with their mothers when they are small. Kenny was "mom's boy" when he was small. In fact, he let out a blood-curdling scream whenever I left him. I tried to help with this by spending a lot of time at home with him in those early years and by thoroughly explaining to him the details of my leaving him. I told him where I was going, when I would be back, and so forth from the time he was barely old enough to understand.

When Kenny became a toddler, he began to go toward his father. I did not fight this; I never intended to be first in Kenny's life. I began gently nudging Kenny toward his dad. However, I also held closely to Kenny, especially when his dad was not around.

B. *Don't give a boy a position of manly leadership when he is too young, even if he seems ready for it.* A young man may feel that he is ready to graduate from high school early, go off to college early, or take a position of ministry early. However, I think it is more beneficial for a man to use those qualities to do servants' tasks. It is not wise for a boy to have the power of a man. He is not old enough emotionally to know how to use it wisely. It is more beneficial for a boy to develop a long and strong foundation in his relationship with his parents.

I understand there is a time when a mother must let go and let her boy become a man, but she should wait until the fruit of her labors is fully ripened. Accept your child's growth in the proper time but avoid the temptation to push your child to do things earlier than other children. Because of Kenny's birthday, my husband and I had a choice of whether to send Kenny to kindergarten a little bit early or a little bit late. We decided to wait a year and send him a little bit late.

C. *Let go of your child a little bit at a time.* I believe the break to go to college should be a big one for a young person, especially for a young man. A wise parent will make a college-age child feel independent. However, he will also stay very aware of what is going on in his child's life. It is hard to know a lot and, at the same time, to refrain from giving advice, but both are important in rearing adult children.

Also, a wise parent will find some way to regularly express his love to his young adult child, even if those ways seem unnoticed and unappreciated. Hugs and kisses should perhaps be less frequent and shorter, especially for boys, but care baskets, funny cards, and kind notes can replace these. I would not make a clean break from an adult child until he is safely down the wedding aisle or at least has graduated from college.

15. Parents talk prematurely about boyfriends, girlfriends, and the intimate marital relationship. My husband and I did not encourage our children to date. Some time in high school, they both began to like a certain someone. We did not forbid this; we even chaperoned a few dates for them, but we did not push their dating. I am against pre-high school dating and am not fond of serious dating until college.

When our teenagers asked about the intimate relationship in marriage, my husband and I tried not to act shocked, and we answered their questions to the degree that we thought they were ready to handle it. We did not push this information on them, however. One month before Jaclynn's wedding, both her father and I discussed things very frankly and thoroughly with her, as well as recommended good books for her to read. We also increased our supervision of her and Todd, rather than decreasing it.

I also would not allow children to wear clothing that is too old for them or that in any way is made to look provocative toward the opposite sex. Let children be children, and innocent ones at that!

16. Parents are unwilling to show weakness around their children. One of the words that Jaclynn and Kenny most often use to describe me is the word "real." I am often told around the country how much people appreciate my "realness."

Human beings love to be perceived as being smart, rich, and successful; women love to be described as being gorgeous and young-looking. I don't think "real" makes the list of most desired attributes. But I love being called "real." Sometimes, when I am told that I am real, I walk away and laugh to myself. "Did they think I was not going to be real? Did they think I would be an alien?" However, I love the word "real," and I love being described as such. I have tried to be real for my children. I want the Cindy Schaap that they see at church to be very much like the Cindy Schaap they see at home.

I have loved the word "real" since I read with my children the book entitled *The Velveteen Rabbit*. The velveteen rabbit belonged to a child. That child had loved it so much that the rabbit had its velvet rubbed off; it looked very old and ugly. But the child loved it so much that the toy rabbit had actually become real to the child.

Though I possess my share of vanity and do not wish to look old and ugly, I realize there is a price to pay for being loved and for being real to a child. The following is part of that price:

A. Say "I am sorry" to your children. From time to time, my mother would come into my bedroom when I was a child to apologize for becoming upset with me. I could become quite exasperating as a child, and she was usually quite patient, but her apologies always warmed my heart.

B. Allow your children to serve you. Refrain from making them think you don't need their help or from doing the job for them. I recall one Mother's Day when my children brought me breakfast in bed. The menu was saltine crackers, cheddar cheese potato chips, chocolate chip cookies, and milk. I ate it all, and it was probably one of my most enjoyable meals.

C. Be willing to show weakness to your children. This was one of my favorite characteristics of my dad. I loved the illustration he gave in church about flushing Reese's Peanut Butter Cups down the toilet of his motel room because he could not resist eating them. Why? Because it made this thunderous preacher, this strong Christian man seem so real. I could relate with his realness (sometimes more than with his spirituality, I'm afraid). Recently, I changed the location of a box of Cheez-its in my cabinets to a place where it would be harder for me to see them because they are such a temptation to me.

I had one person say to me about my dad's Reese's experience, "I bet the plumber at the motel didn't appreciate that!" (I don't remember who this person was. It's a good thing because I would describe this person as being very "unreal.") That's the whole point! He did something he should not have done, and he was willing to admit it!

D. Do not show shock or anger when your children share their innermost thoughts with you. Both Jaclynn and Kenny have come to me at times in their lives to share with me some feelings of self-doubt or temptation. Most often, I have responded by telling them of a time when I was their age when I felt that same temptation or experienced that same self-doubt. I believe this is what has kept the communication so open between us and what has kept me real to them.

Remember, to get people to treat you the way you want them to, you must first set the example. If you want your husband and children to open up to you, you must first make yourself vulnerably open to them. That is a price you pay for being real!

E. You be the determiner of what you reveal about yourself. Sometimes I feel almost embarrassed about my transparency when I write or speak, but I continue to be real. Why? Because I want to help you. I would not waste my time speaking or writing if it were to impress you. We both have too many other things to do with our time. I want to help you! I want you to feel loved, and to do this, I must shed some of my velvet.

Believe it or not, there are scores of things I have chosen not to reveal about myself. I have nothing to hide, so I am willing to open my closet door for all the world to see. However, only two get to go with me all the way inside the closet—God and my husband. Yes, they know things about me that I would not want you to know, nor allow you to know. But if you should come all the way into my closet, you would find that I am made of flesh; you would find that I am very much like you!

Perhaps I have waited till the end of this list of "Common Mistakes Parents Make" to share what should have been at the beginning of this list. I'm not sure there is anything more important in communication, in child rearing, or in any other relationship than being real.

As I grow older, I may color my hair or it may turn to gray; I may watch my weight or I may get pleasantly plump; I may grow wiser or I may grow more forgetful; I may be rich or I may be poor; I may seem successful to the world or I may seem like a failure; but most of all, I wish it to be true that I am still real…and when I see Jesus, I hope He will see in me someone who is familiar, and I hope He will see someone who is real.

CONCLUSION

I made a lot of mistakes when I was rearing my children—as much as any mom, I suppose. But I have no regrets. I have learned that mistakes and regrets feel very different. Young mothers, please heed the advice of a mother gone before: invest your time, even your life, in making your home a happy place and in guarding it from the Devil who seeks to destroy it! Let's enjoy, let's train, and let's protect our children!

COMMON MISTAKES MADE IN CHILD REARING:

Parents have no vision for their children
Parents have too much vision for their children.
Parents have too much concern for their own reputation.
Parents do not use enough positive methods in child rearing.
Parents do not provide enough private time for their children.
Parents do not have enough fun interaction with their children.
Parents allow their children to watch too much television.
Parents depend too much on the Christian school to rear their children.
Parents do not require their children to do enough work.
Parents allow their children to have too much idle time and/or too much time with their peers.
Parents do not promote clear leadership in the home.
Parents do not have proper priorities in the home.
Parents do not show enough clear support for the authorities in their children's lives.
Parents push children to grow up too soon.
Parents talk prematurely about boyfriends, girlfriends, and the intimate marital relationship.
Parents are unwilling to show weakness around their children.

8

How to Stay Close to Your Teenagers

My father was the pastor of a mega church for 41 years. He also founded and superintended a college, two grade schools, two junior high schools, and two high schools. He traveled and counseled extensively. This description only begins to portray how busy he was.

The week that my father was in the hospital following a heart attack and preceding his death, our church people did us a great favor. They let our family have my dad to ourselves. This was something that rarely happened. Other than family, only a few people actually stayed at the hospital that week. There was a group of security guards from our church who took turns standing vigil in a very professional way. And there was my father's dear friend and assistant pastor, Dr. Ray Young.

I'm not sure Dr. Young ever left the hospital the week my dad was there, but I know that he never interfered with our family. He didn't try to go into the room to see my father; he was just there. My respect for this man, as well as for our security guards, grew immensely during that week. I understood, maybe for the first time, how much they loved Dad.

As I have thought of the subject of staying close to your teenagers, I have thought of two things Dr. Young did that illustrate what a parent is to be to a teenager and adult child.

1. **Always be there.** In order to be close to a teenager, you must chase after him. A grade school child's schedule is predictable and sim-

ple. The child can build his schedule around yours. He arrives home from school, has a snack, plays alone and with mom, does his homework, eats supper, and gets ready for bed. He may not do it in that order, but that is pretty much the schedule of every grade school child; it's nice and convenient for mother.

Then come the teen years which are filled with extracurricular activities and practices. Mom is a taxi driver, running here and there. She never seems to know what to expect. Mom should no longer expect her children to fit into her schedule; she must fit into theirs.

I thought that I would be less busy as my children grew, but when they started junior high school, I realized I would be busier than ever. I was doing a bit of traveling and speaking on the home but cancelled all of my speaking engagements and spent most of my time on gymnasium bleachers. I don't know that I ever missed an activity where either of my children was playing or performing. I have no regrets!

I also drove the children to most of their activities. We talked a lot in the car, and I found pleasure in driving them places. I rarely complained about being their taxi driver; I saw it as quality time to be together.

2. Interfere as little as possible. A good parent of teenagers knows when to be there and how to get lost. Parenting a teenager can be a thankless task. They need you to be around, especially to chaperone their dates, but they don't always want you to be around. I did a lot of chaperoning when Jaclynn was dating Todd. One of the favorite places to go was a certain bookstore in the area that has a coffee shop. I would go with them to the bookstore so that I could chaperone them. But I would sit by myself at the coffee shop, while Jaclynn and Todd sat at another table. I did this so they could be alone.

A few years after Jaclynn was married, she mentioned that she thought a certain young man was struggling. "Mom," she said, "this young man goes to bookstores and sits in the coffee shop by himself by the hour; isn't that strange?"

"I don't think it's strange," I replied. "I used to do that when I was chaperoning you and Todd." We both got a good laugh out of that, and I was reminded of the sometimes unglamorous job of parenting a teenager. Now Todd and Jaclynn are married and live just a mile away from our house with their two children. I still try to be there if they need me, but I try not to interfere. I rarely call their house, especially if Todd is there, but Jaclynn often calls me. I do not drop by their house unannounced. I am rarely at their house just hanging out with Jaclynn if Todd is home. Jaclynn comes to my house more than I come to hers.

Some Additional Ideas for Staying Close to Teenagers

1. Never expect your children to meet your needs; you meet their needs. II Corinthians 12:14, 15, *"Behold, the third time I am ready to come to you; and I will not be burdensome to you: for I seek not your's, but you: for the children ought not to lay up for the parents, but the parents for the children. And I will very gladly spend and be spent for you; though the more abundantly I love you, the less I be loved."*

Properly trained children are so much fun that if we are not careful, we will start leaning upon them to nurture us. I never call Jaclynn to pick me up if I am having a bad day. I may call my mother, but I don't call my daughter. Jaclynn may call me if she is having a bad day. I want to remain the parent in the situation.

Children do have a responsibility, according to the Bible, to honor their parents, but the parent should not expect honor. This should be a decision between the child and God.

Sometimes when Jaclynn comments on a favor my husband and I have done for her, I remind her that our payback will come when she does the same thing for her children.

2. Love your children with no strings attached. On occasion my husband and I have been able to meet a large monetary need of our children. We always make sure that all money is given with no strings attached. We don't buy their love or make them feel indebted to us. We have given money, but we haven't loaned it.

3. Don't make your children your whole world. Many mothers neglect their marriage and their personal lives in order to fulfill themselves solely through their children. Those same mothers will probably eventually push away their children by trying to suffocate them with their love when the child is trying to pull away.

4.   Don't look back. In my day-to-day living, I frequently come across mothers who are enjoying their small children. A twinge of sentimentality may grip my soul. But I quickly let go of that sentimentality and remind myself that I once had the opportunity to rear small children. I enjoyed that stage, but now that stage is over. For the sake of my children, I don't look back.

5.   Treat them more like an adult than a child. Most of the training should be done when the children are small. The teen years should be mainly affirming years, and the adult years should be completely affirming years. A teenager is more adult than child, and an adult will always respond negatively to another adult's criticism. Overcorrecting of a teen is probably a result of poor training during childhood.

Once a child reaches adult stage, you have done all the training you can. Now you must live with the results. If their room is messy, I would let it be messy. Once they are out on their own, they will probably adapt to a more clean lifestyle. Other than keeping track of their whereabouts, very little correcting should be done to an adult child, even if they live at home.

6.   Affirm them. A teenager and adults don't need to hear how much you know. They need to know that you believe in them and in what they know.

7.   Give little advice and criticism. I only give advice to our adult children if they ask me, and there are some subjects about which I hesitate to give advice even then.

8.   Don't compete with them. I remember getting myself ready for an event, thinking I looked pretty fine, then going downstairs and seeing our beautiful teenage daughter, and then thinking, "I need to go back to the mirror and try a little harder." My daughter is not only gorgeous, she is also 21 years younger than I am. She is one of our church pianists and is, in some ways, more in demand than I am. But I am proud of her. I made a commitment many years ago that I would never be jealous of Jaclynn or compete with her.

9.   Don't have too high of expectations for your children. Many parents struggle with their teenage children because they expect them to earn straight A's, excel on the basketball court, or be popular. These parents are living their lives through their teenagers, which is a serious mistake. Keep your vision for your children general. Have an "outline" goal for them to be happy and to serve the Lord. But let God color in the lines of their lives.

10. **Love their friends.** I remember saying something critical about one of Kenny's friends. I could tell by the look on his face that I had made a mistake. I am not talking about letting your children hang around with the wrong crowd. But many parents find fault with all of their children's peers. They alienate their children from their peers. Your children's friends will not be perfect saints of God. Many times our problem with our children's friends is not really a result of the quality of their lives, but rather a sign of our superior and critical spirit.

11. **PRAY! PRAY! PRAY! PRAY! PRAY!** Though I do not give unsought advice to our adult children, I do pray about EVERY aspect of their lives, their ministries, their marriages, and their child rearing. Prayer is not only the number-one ingredient to rearing good children; it is also the number-one way to keep ourselves from interfering in our children's lives.

12. **Establish a good foundation in the baby/child years.** If I were to pile a stack of several books and one of the top books fell off, the stack would remain in place. But if I were to remove the bottom or the foundational book, the whole stack would fall apart. So it is with child rearing. Most parents experience some shaky days with their children when they are teenagers. But if they have established a good foundation in childhood, the relationship will eventually become right again. Establish a good foundation of training and love in child rearing so that the teenage years can be enjoyable ones. And in summary, remember to always be there—but interfere as little as possible.

9

HELPING REBELLIOUS CHILDREN

I went through a time of rebellion starting in my junior high school years and culminating during my sophomore year of high school. Though I have never tasted alcohol, never smoked a cigarette, never attended a movie, and never really got into any kind of rock music, I was still rebellious. I had a smart mouth, was disruptive in my school classrooms, and I received 123 demerits during my sophomore year. My grades were much lower than they should have been. I never failed a class, but I could have done much better than I did. I was suspended from school for a day.

My rebellion was not against my parents. Rather, I was rebellious against some circumstances in my life. I was a preacher's kid, and I did not feel that I was very good at it. During my junior year, God completely changed my life. One year later I made straight A's in school and had no demerits. I would like to share with you some lessons I learned during my own personal experience with rebellion.

Though I look back and see my rebellion as my own fault and no one else's, I do recall instances of adult behavior which both increased and decreased my rebellion.

HOW TO PROMOTE REBELLION

1. Take out your moods on your children. Though my parents were not guilty of this, I remember watching some authority figures taking out their bad moods on other children. I have always hated to see people treated unjustly to a fault. Even as a child, I could see the injustice of children's being mistreated because of an authority's mood, and though it was only my own sin which caused my rebellion, I do believe that this type of injustice enhanced it.

I have mentioned in a previous chapter to only spank your children because of planned reasons, and I listed the seven reasons why we spanked our children. One should never spank a child because of inconvenience or because one is in a bad mood. This will definitely cause rebellion down the road.

2. Treat rebels with disrespect. Children who break rules must be punished, but there is never a time to treat them with disrespect.

I recall a teacher in high school who pounded on my desk and screamed, "You will obey in this class. I don't care who you are." I believe that I deserved every bit of punishment I received during my time of rebellion, but I also believe to this day the disrespect I received was wrong.

3. Consider children to be arrogant because of their status in life. Whenever a person achieves a position of status or, I should say, a position that people deem to be of status, it is common for that person to be written off as arrogant and then to receive mistreatment.

It has been said, and I believe, that we hate in others what we fight in ourselves. People who mistreat children because of the strengths or the position of their parents are not showing the arrogance of the child, but rather their own arrogance.

4. Ignore children because of their strengths or weaknesses. It is common to ignore the best kid in the class because we don't want to make him the teacher's pet. Instead of making him the teacher's pet, we ignore him and make him pay for his good behavior or for the position of his parent in society.

It is also common to ignore the child who gets on our nerves and whose weaknesses are hard to tolerate. When we do this, we are having our part in training a future rebel.

How to Heal Rebellion

1. Guard the self-esteem of your children. I try to treat people on the premise of this fact: I believe that 99.9 percent of people are insecure, and I'm not sure I have met the 0.1 percent who are secure. Therefore, in all of my dealings with people, I must guard the self-esteem of each person with whom I come in contact. Especially if your child is a rebel, you should build your child's confidence and not compare him with others.

2. Praise the rebellious child. The day I was suspended from school, my dad took me shopping and bought me a spring coat. When I have shared with others what my dad did, others have questioned, "Wasn't your dad rewarding you for doing wrong?" The truth is that I had so many authorities on my case at this time and deservedly so, that I was barely surviving.

The day after I was suspended from school, I found a book on my mother's shelf about self-esteem. It was entitled *I Hate Myself!* I was only 15 years old, and I was a smart aleck, but those three words in that title described how I felt. I took the book off of my mother's shelf, walked to the park, and read it.

I had one really neat person who not only loved me; he also liked me. I was convinced of that. He was my father and my pastor, and he made all of the difference in the world. He consistently told me what was good about me. He saved my life from being one of rebellion.

3. Point out the assets and the liabilities of the rebel's personality. The day I was suspended from school, my dad told me two things that I have never forgotten.

> A. He described one of my greatest assets. "You are a very just person, and you love deeply." I had been suspended for arguing with a teacher about the way she had treated another student. I was wrong in the way I handled it, but I do believe the student was being treated unjustly. My dad's praise gave me an identity.

B. He described my liability concisely and directly. "You need to learn to keep your mouth shut."

Dad never once mentioned how he and Mom felt about my being in trouble. They did not make their feelings the issue. To them, I was the issue.

4. **Give the rebellious child a way out.** Don't back a child into a corner. When Dad said, "You need to keep your mouth shut," I thought, "I can do that!" I did not feel useless like I did before I talked to Dad. I felt I had great redeeming value. I just needed to do one thing—shut my mouth when I didn't agree with a person's justice.

As I have already stated, the problem was definitely my own wicked sin of rebellion, but I couldn't have taken having my hero pointing that out to me at that moment. Dad knew I was too down on myself. Dad gave me a way out.

That is one reason that I share so many of my weaknesses in my writing. It is not always fun to do so; sometimes it leaves me feeling vulnerable. But when I try to correct other people's weaknesses by relating to my own, it gives them the confidence they need to change. I often shared with our children some weakness I experienced at their age when they came to me with confessions. Sometimes I wanted to act shocked, alarmed, and maybe even angry. Instead, I tried to calmly confess a similar experience so as to help preserve their self dignity and motivate them to change.

5. **Spend time with your children.** It wasn't the spring coat that I needed when Dad took me shopping the day I was suspended; it was Dad's time. And Dad was there with his time again and again and again. He also showed me through the shopping experience that life was good and would go on even during the worst of times.

6. **Point the rebellious child to good friends.** You can't make your child hang around with good kids; this too can cause rebellion, but I know that God used good friends to help me out of my personal rebellion. God used four sisters who sang together—Teresa, Robyn, Karen, and Connie Foster—to help me. They moved into our area and joined our church just as I was really needing some friends who weren't ashamed to talk about the Lord. Robyn, in particular, and her mother,

Barbara Foster, were greatly used of God to draw me closer to God and to build my self-esteem. I haven't seen them in many years, but I think about them often.

My father, Dr. Jack Hyles, often said, "No child would turn out bad if he had one person who really cared about him." For me, that person was Dr. Jack Hyles. I never rebelled against my father. I am now 46 years old, and my father has been in Heaven for five years. I have no obligation to try to please my father, but I don't think a day goes by that I don't think about what he would have me to do if he were here. If Dad were here, I would tell him, "Because of you, I am still not rebelling, I am still trying to do what is right, and I am still trying to keep my mouth shut."

10

HOW TO FIND
THE RIGHT SPOUSE

When Jaclynn was a senior in high school, she expressed a desire to date a young man named Todd Weber. To be honest with you, I was concerned with Jaclynn's desire. Though I knew of Todd's family and knew they were fine people, I did not know them well, and I did not know much about Todd at all. All I knew about Todd was that he was an excellent basketball player (Todd lived in Michigan and played on a rival team of Jaclynn's school)and that, in Jaclynn's and my opinion, he was tall, dark, and handsome. I did know one other thing about Todd. He had received a scholarship to play basketball at a state university, and he was considering accepting that scholarship.

Jaclynn had surrendered to full-time Christian service, so I questioned her desire to date a basketball star. I did not tell Jaclynn my fears, but in my mind I wondered, "Did I rear a shallow daughter?" I expressed my negative feelings to Jaclynn, and then I decided to "shut up" about it.

The summer after Jaclynn's senior year, she came to me and said, "Mom, I have a strong desire to meet the man I am supposed to marry very soon." Though Jaclynn was still young, I understood her desire. I too had been impatient in meeting "Mr. Right." I prayed and met my husband when I was just 17. We dated until one year before I graduated from college, and then we got married.

197

I challenged Jaclynn to fast and pray all summer that God would lead her to the man she was supposed to marry. I myself was terribly concerned about Jaclynn's marrying God's choice for her. I did not want Jaclynn to waste a lot of time dating guys she would not marry. I had dated around a lot and saw it as a waste of time.

Jaclynn promised to pray and fast about finding God's choice. Unbeknownst to Todd, while he was practicing with the Valparaiso University basketball team that summer, Jaclynn was praying and fasting that he would come to Hyles-Anderson College. I have no doubt that his parents, pastor, and youth leaders were praying also. Yet I wonder what would have happened if Jaclynn had not been praying and fasting.

I took a lot of long summer walks and begged God to help Jaclynn to make the right choices in her dating. I did not pray about Todd, however, because my heart was not in it.

On Jaclynn's first day of college, she saw Todd Weber on campus, and they became the best of friends. Her dating around in college was short and merely a formality. She just could not keep her mind off of Todd Weber. The first thing Jaclynn mentioned about Todd when she started dating him was this: "Mom, Todd really seems to walk with God."

I, as Jaclynn's mother, had been wrong about Todd. He is more than tall, dark, and handsome. He is a wonderful Christian man who has made an excellent husband, father, and son-in-law. I was also wrong about Jaclynn; she is not one bit shallow in her Christian life and in her walk with God, and she was not one bit shallow in choosing the husband who is God's will for her.

A popular theory is going around Christian circles these days that parents should choose their children's spouses. I teasingly say that children should allow their mothers to choose their spouse according to whose mother she likes the best. I have no desire to go on a crusade disputing the "courtship" theory. But I would like to share my story as a testimony of how to help your children choose a mate.

The story of Isaac's marrying Rebekah in Genesis chapter 24 is sometimes used to support the theory that parents should choose their children's spouses. I would like to use the same story to share my beliefs about the subject.

TEACHING YOUR CHILD HIS ROLE

1.   **First of all, I believe that the Lord has appointed one particular person for your child to marry.** I have no doubt that my appointed one was Jack Schaap, that Jaclynn's appointed one was Todd Weber and that Kenny Schaap's appointed one was Candace Hooker, who is now his wife. Genesis 24:44b, *"…let the same be the woman whom the Lord hath appointed out for my master's son."*

2.   **The Holy Spirit of God is to lead your child to the right spouse.** I believe the servant in Genesis 24 represents the Holy Spirit. Notice that the only living parent, Abraham, never met Rebekah until after she had been chosen as Isaac's wife. The servant found Rebekah.

Genesis 24:7c, *"…he shall send his angel before thee, and thou shalt take a wife unto my son from thence."*

Genesis 24:40, *"And he said unto me, The LORD, before whom I walk, will send his angel with thee, and prosper thy way; and thou shalt take a wife for my son of my kindred, and of my father's house."*

Genesis 24:56b, *"…seeing the Lord hath prospered my way…."*

As a pastor, my husband has had to settle many arguments between parents and children about chosen spouses. Many parents are convinced that a particular young man or lady is the one for their child. There is just one problem: their child is not at all attracted to that young man or lady. A lot of unnecessary strife develops, and hearts are unnecessarily broken.

When I was questioning Jaclynn's interest in Todd, my pastor father gave me this advice. "Let Jaclynn choose her spouse. If you choose him and things don't work out, you will feel responsible, and it will be harder for you to help Jaclynn." That was wise advice!

3.   **The parents should teach their child how to walk with God and how to make decisions.** The most important lesson my parents taught me and the most important lesson we taught Jaclynn and Kenny is to walk with God. At a young age, Jaclynn developed an amazing walk with God, and that relationship led her to God's will for her life.

Not only did my husband and I insist that our children have private Bible reading and prayer time, but we also taught them how to make decisions on their own. Many times one of our children would ask my husband to make a decision for them, and he would refuse. Instead, he would give them guidelines for making that decision, and he would encourage them to make it themselves.

4.   The parents should teach their child to start at a young age praying that God would lead him to marry the right spouse. I began praying when I was in high school, and maybe even sooner, that God would lead me to my spouse. Our children did the same. I am sure that I had prayed dozens of prayers regarding our children's marrying the right spouse by the time they married. All the way up to Jaclynn's and Kenny's engagement, I prayed that God would show them if they were dating the wrong one for their lives. This gave me peace and kept me from interfering. And I am convinced God answered my prayer and caused them to marry the spouses who are God's perfect will for their lives.

Abraham's asking the servant (the Holy Spirit) to find Isaac's mate represents the parents' important role of praying and not interfering in their child's dating. Genesis 24:12, *"And he said, O LORD God of my master Abraham, I pray thee, send me good speed this day, and shew kindness unto my master Abraham."*

5.   A parent should teach his child that if he is doing God's will, God will lead him to the spouse he is supposed to marry. Genesis 24:27c, *"...I being in the way, the LORD led me...."* The servant asked God to send an angel before him and prepare the way. Having done this, the servant was in the right place at the right time to find Rebekah.

TEACHING YOUR CHILD WHAT TO LOOK FOR IN A SPOUSE

1.   Teach your child to look for a separated Christian. Abraham sent his servant back to his homeland to find a wife for Isaac. He did not want Isaac to marry one of the heathen girls of Canaan. Genesis 24:2-4, *"And Abraham said unto his eldest servant of his house, that ruled over all* that he had, Put, I pray thee, thy hand under my thigh: And I will make thee swear by the LORD, the God of heaven, and the God of the earth, that thou shalt not take a wife unto my son of the daughters of the Canaanites, among whom I dwell: But thou shalt go unto my country, and to my kindred, and take a wife unto my son Isaac." Teach your child early not to even consider dating someone who is unsaved or worldly.

2. **Teach your child to look for a hard worker.** Rebekah gave drink to Abraham's servant and to his servants and all of their camels. In order to do this, she had to make several trips to the water well, carrying several heavy pots of water back and forth on her head.

3. **Teach your child to look for a spouse with a servant's heart.** Camels drink a lot of water! Much can be consumed in just one gulp. It was a servant's heart that caused Rebekah to offer this gesture to a stranger and then to fulfill it.

4. **Teach your child to look for a spouse who has a desire to do God's will.** Genesis 24:58 says, *"And they called Rebekah, and said unto her, Wilt thou go with this man? And she said, I will go."* Rebekah must have had a great desire to do God's will. Don't expect your child to date someone who is perfect but someone who desires to do God's will.

5. **Teach your child to look for a spouse who walks with God.** Genesis 24:63a, *"And Isaac went out to meditate in the field at the eventide…."* A person who walks with God will always be growing in his maturity as a Christian.

What Is the Parents' Role in Their Child's Dating?

1. **The parents should have the role of veto power in their child's dating.** I teach the students at Hyles-Anderson College how important it is for them to get their parents involved in getting to know the young man they are dating. I admonish them to give their parents the authority to tell them "no" if they believe the young man is not right for their daughter.

Parents must take this responsibility soberly. They must take their own selfish desires out of the equation and must prayerfully consider what is best for the child and, most of all, what is God's will. A submissive wife will look to her Christian husband to approve or veto her child's choice of a mate. A wife should not allow herself to get so emotionally involved in her child's dating that she develops a strong will in the matter. I have known mothers to fight their daughter's decision to break up with a young man because the mother was emotionally attached to him.

    2. The parents' role is to sanction God's will. Rebekah's parents said in Genesis 24:50, *"Then Laban and Bethuel answered and said, This thing proceedeth from the Lord: we cannot speak unto thee bad or good."* In other words, this is the will of God, and our opinion should not even be spoken.

    3. The parents' role is to let go of their child. Genesis 24:51, *"Behold, Rebekah is before thee, take her, and go, and let her be thy master's son's wife, as the Lord hath spoken."* Remember, there were no cars, trains, airplanes, telephones, or e-mail in those days. It is likely that Laban and Bethuel never saw their daughter on earth again. Yet they let Rebekah leave their home with this stranger. Why? Because the Lord had spoken to them. God's will seemed to be the only issue in their daughter's marriage.

    I have known many mothers who sanctioned their sons to marry, believing it was God's will, but then refused to let go. They would not completely cut the apron strings. If their son did not visit them every other weekend, his wife was made to feel that she had somehow wronged her in-laws by taking away their son. Genesis 2:24, *"Therefore shall a man leave his father and mother, and shall cleave unto his wife: and they shall be one flesh."*

    Ephesians 5:31, *"For this cause shall a man leave his father and mother, and shall be joined unto his wife, and they two shall be one flesh."*

    A married child should be afforded to choose when he spends time with his parents and where he lives. The parents' job is to let go.

    4. The parents' role is to give their child their blessing. Genesis 24:60, *"And they blessed Rebekah, and said unto her, Thou art our sister, be thou the mother of thousands of millions, and let thy seed possess the gate of those which hate them."* How sad is the number of parents who refuse to attend their child's wedding because they weren't allowed to choose their mate. Even if parents strongly feel their child is marrying against God's will, those parents should give their unconditional love and attend the wedding. Then the children will come to them when they have marriage problems or should their spouse leave them. Once you have stated your veto power, you have no more power with your adult children than to pray for them and to love them.

TEACH YOUR CHILD THE RESULT OF MARRYING IN GOD'S WILL

1. The result of marrying in God's will is physical attraction. Teach your children that God will not make them marry someone to whom they are not attracted, and neither will you, by the way. Genesis 24:64, *"And Rebekah lifted up her eyes, and when she saw Isaac, she lighted off the camel."* This does not sound like a partner in a forced marriage. Rebekah had a desire to be near Isaac.

2. The result of marrying in God's will is love and comfort. Genesis 24:67, *"And Isaac brought her into his mother Sarah's tent, and took Rebekah, and she became his wife; and he loved her: and Isaac was comforted after his mother's death."* Marriage outside of God's will is less than comforting. It is full of strife and bickering that often leads to divorce. True love exists in a marriage where two people are joined by God's will. I must say that my 27-year marriage to my husband has been a great comfort to me. And our children's marriages have been a great comfort to us also, as I am sure they have been to them.

CONCLUSION

There is nothing more comforting than to see your children involved in a marriage where they are one with God's will for their lives—unless it is to be involved in such a marriage yourself. Genesis 24:48 says, *"And I bowed down my head, and worshipped the LORD, and blessed the LORD God of my master Abraham, which had led me in the right way to take my master's brother's daughter unto his son."* Praise the Lord for His leadership in that wonderful institution called marriage!

11

A MOTHER'S LOVE

Several years ago I watched some old home movies with many of my family members. These movies were taken when I was less than a year old. The movies showed my parents kissing me, playing with me, and "gootchey-gooing" (as my father would say) with me. It was obvious as I watched my parents caring for me that I was a lot of trouble and that they absolutely adored me. It is amazing how much that "gootchey-gooing" meant to me as I watched those movies, even though I was already an adult with my own children. How blessed I am to have known the love of two wonderful parents. And how adoring and selfless is the love of a parent, particularly that of a mother.

I enjoy looking at my own family albums and remembering how much I enjoyed the babyhood of my own two children. As I see pictures of me holding Jaclynn and Kenny on my lap, I see behind my own smile the tremendous joy I felt in rearing them. The love we shared during their childhood days was not only a precious gift from God; it was just plain fun! My husband and I were the center of their little universe; and in some respects, they were the center of ours.

Unfortunately, through some of my counseling, I have observed mothers and children who seem to have become hostile enemies to each other.

In June of 2002 as I prepared for Jaclynn to leave our home, I made some decisions to help maintain our friendship throughout all of our lifetime. Even more importantly, I want Jaclynn to rest secure in her mother's love.

A Letter to Jaclynn on Her Wedding Day

Allow me to share with you a letter I wrote as I prepared for Jaclynn's wedding.

Dear Jaclynn,

1. *I promise to be available when you and Todd need me.* In spite of a busy schedule, my dad had an uncanny ability of always being there when I needed him. But I must admit, when I didn't need him, he was very hard to find.

2. *I promise to "get lost" when that is what you and Todd want or need from me.*

3. *I promise not to give unsought advice or criticism.* I promise to say the sweetest words a daughter can hear from a mother: "I am proud of you!" I will say them over and over. (I **am** proud of you, Jaclynn— very proud!)

4. *I promise to affirm you.* Though I have not yet seen your first home, I have already decided it is beautiful and immaculately clean (or clean enough for me). I have not yet eaten in your home, but your cooking is already delicious.

5. *I promise not to compete with you.* I will always want the biggest and the best that is in God's will for you. And to every new achievement or to every new purchase, I promise to respond with a mother's love.

6. *I promise to be pleased with each accomplishment that seems less than what others may have expected.* I know you want to do God's will, and I know He will use you in great ways, though they may be big or small.

7. *I promise to be pleased with your plans, whether they bring you closer to me or take you further away.*

8. *I promise never to come between you and Todd.*

9. *I promise to take Todd's side.* (I'm sorry, dear, but a promise is a promise, and I already made it.)

10. *I promise to affirm your choice of a spouse.* To you Todd is a knight in shining armor, and, to me, he is too. I promise that when I find chinks

in the armor, I will just keep looking only at the shining spots. I will remember that Todd will be one flesh with you and that to criticize him is to criticize you.

11. *I promise that when you drive off after your wedding, I will look to my own knight in shining armor* (your father), *and I promise to live happily ever after.*

Jaclynn, I know that these promises are more easily made than kept. But just as I expect you to keep your vows to Todd " 'til death do you part," I promise to keep these vows to you " 'til death do us part." Should I find it difficult to keep these vows, I will simply look into my heart and find where I have lost my mother's love. Then I will find it again. Because I do love you, Jaclynn—with no strings attached—with a mother's love.

Congratulations, Jaclynn, with all of my best wishes! I'm proud of you, and I'm proud of Todd!

Love,

Your Mother

UNIT FIVE

LESSONS FOR MOTHERS

1

MY PERFECT IMAGE

I recently read a story that touched my heart. A young couple had two children. The oldest was a healthy boy, and the youngest was a mildly retarded girl. When the daughter Molly was about two, the couple sent her away. They did not tell their son where she went. They simply said, "Molly is living somewhere else; she is happy, and you are not allowed to talk about her anymore."

The little boy never forgot his sister Molly, however. When he became an adult, he learned that Molly had been sent away to an institution. She had lived under the care of a supervisor who tended to over 60 children each day. Molly had spent most of her formative years lying all day in a bed amongst several babies, with no family to love her.

When she was an adult, Molly's big brother found her. At that time she was living in a smaller group home. Molly's brother and his wife visited her every week and took her to several fun places. While they were visiting Molly, a doctor informed the brother that his sister was not really that retarded. Had she been trained well in a real home, she could have lived a more normal life. As it turned out, she had the mind and abilities of a preschool child.

Molly's brother also discovered that his father had taken a side job as a clown so that he could go into the institution to see how Molly was doing. Molly's grandmother secretly visited Molly every week and played with her. What explanation was given for Molly's being given away?

Her father worked in an executive position. Her mother often entertained other executives and their families in her home. She did not want Molly to embarrass her and to ruin her perfect image.

I went to bed with a heavy heart after reading this story, and I thought about it much of the next day. I did not feel angry at this mother whom I have never met. I cannot really know her motives. Instead, I felt grieved at all of the selfishness I see in my life and in those around me as we strive to convey that "perfect image." Allow me to share some of those thoughts with you.

1.   We cook an elaborate meal on the holiday because we want everything to be picture perfect; then we snap at our families because we are so worn out.

2.   We try to make our house look as impressive as the Joneses' next door; then we treat our children as if they are in the way when they sit down in our living room.

3.   We move into houses that we can barely afford; then we place our children in a baby sitter's care so that we can keep the bills paid.

4.   We become bored with being home alone with our children, so we choose a career that will fulfill us and sacrifice our best training years with our children.

5.   We make our decisions based on what will give us a good identity amongst our peers at church or in the neighborhood, rather than based on God's priorities for our lives or what is best for our husband and children.

I must admit that at some point in my life, I have been guilty of some of this. As I read my own writing, I am wanting to say a great big "OUCH!" But it is necessary sometimes to stop and refocus on what is important. For some of you, a simple refocus is all that is needed. For many American women, a complete lifestyle change is more in order. As an empty nester, let me say, "Please do your best with your children; they grow up so quickly!" Yet, as you do your best, remember you will never be perfect. No one is really perfect at anything.

I believe in being first-class. I believe in giving God my best. I believe in the goal of giving my family the best I can as their maid, their cook, and their chief bottle washer. I believe in being as first-class as I can afford to be. And I believe in being as first-class as I can without running over people.

As I have thought today of the Mollys of this world, I have been reminded of Isaiah 49:15, *"Can a woman forget her sucking child, that she should not have compassion on the son of her womb? yea, they may forget, yet will I not forget thee."*

No love is as steadfast as a mother's love. Yet the rising abortion rate in this country is proof that mothers sometimes do forget their own. How thankful I am that we have a Saviour Who never forgets. My prayer is that I will forget my "perfect image" and love others more as Jesus has loved me.

2

THE PURPOSE OF A FAMILY

"Lo, children are an heritage of the LORD: and the fruit of the womb is his reward. As arrows are in the hand of a mighty man; so are children of the youth." (Psalm 127:3, 4) In the many families with which my husband and I have counseled, I have seen two extremes. First, there is the family that does not take enough priority in the lives of its members. Secondly, there is the family that is so close that they seem to have lost touch with what is God's purpose for a family. Being close becomes the end and not the means to their goal.

In my family, balance is my goal. I have strived to encourage closeness in my own family unit. I have strived to stay close to our children. The Bible teaches us that children are like arrows. An arrow is not merely a possession; it has a purpose. But all good hunters know that arrows must be maintained. An arrow must be cleaned and sharpened. If a hunter doesn't know where his arrows are, or if he neglects his arrows, his arrows probably will not be very useful.

So it is with children and families. They must be watched over, cared for, and yes, enjoyed, or they will not grow to be useful in accomplishing their purpose. A family is a precious gift from God that should be valued and held dear. Time together as a family should be a frequent and cherished event. I believe with all of my heart that God intended us to have close families. The purpose, however, of a family is not to be close.

I have a close relationship with my own husband and children. I am one of those wives who would really love to be with my husband all of the time. There have not been too many days during the 27 years of our marriage when I have not felt some sadness when my husband left to go to work. You might ask, "With an attitude like that, how have you managed to be married to a pastor of such a large church?" I have tried to remember the purpose of our marriage.

Brother Troy Blackwell once said, **"When the possession of something becomes more important than its purpose, then that something becomes an idol."** I wrote down that saying in the back of my Bible and have tried to remember it. When my possession of a wonderful husband, marriage, and family becomes more important than its purpose, then that husband, marriage, or family becomes an idol.

What then is the purpose of the family? Psalm 34:3 says, *"O magnify the LORD with me, and let us exalt his name together."* My husband and I read this verse together several times when we were dating, and this is a verse which has come to mind several times in the last 27 years. The purpose of a family is to magnify the Lord. A marriage is to magnify the Lord, and it should also bring forth children who will be honed into sharp, useful arrows to be used in spiritual battle for the Lord.

A few months ago my daughter Jaclynn asked me, "Mom, have you ever **not** wanted to be in full-time Christian work?" I chuckled to myself thinking of how many times in my life I have truly **not** wanted to be in full-time Christian work as I should. But I answered Jaclynn something like this: "Jaclynn, yes, I have not wanted to serve the Lord—lots of times. But my father, your grandfather, served the Lord when he did not want to. Grandpa Hyles really wished for a simple life. He often stated he would like to have had a 9-to-5 job in a small town. He would like to have lived in a house with a white picket fence on Main Street. But that was not God's will for him." (Brother Hyles was a simple person, and so am I. I often tease to my husband that I am a simple girl working in a very complicated ministry.)

"Jaclynn," I added, "God's will was for your grandfather to provide a church, a Christian school, and a college for people like us, not to mention all of the other numerous programs we enjoy at First Baptist

Church of Hammond—programs such as the youth baseball league, cheerleading squads, etc. God's will was for Grandpa Hyles to travel each week trying to keep our country free for my generation."

"Yes, Jaclynn, I have not wanted to serve God from time to time, but I just don't feel that I can take what has been provided for me and then say to yours and Kenny's generation, 'Who cares about you? You are on your own. I don't **want** to be in full-time Christian work. I want to enjoy my wonderful husband, my wonderful marriage, and my wonderful family.' Jaclynn, if I am just, I must pay my debt to do my part to provide for you what my father provided for me. Fortunately for me, I am married to a man with the same vision.'"

Now through the ministries the Lord has given, my husband and I are privileged to try to pay our debt to the previous generation through the next generation. I see First Baptist Church of Hammond, the church my husband pastors, as a tool through which God has provided us an opportunity to magnify the Lord to a nation and to a world, and as tools to show the next generation what Jack and Beverly Hyles and Ken and Marlene Schaap have taught us, as well as what others have taught us. Of course, soul winning is the ultimate method through which we magnify God.

My desire is that those women who read this book would be the kind of ladies who have close families. We need women who sacrifice their own agenda to provide watch care for their husband and children. But we also need women who know when to let go. We need women who will allow their husbands to serve the Lord. We need women who will let go of their children when it is time to let go. We need women who realize that we must divide before we can multiply. We need to allow our children to start their own close families and to do what is God's will for them, all the while reminding them that we are here if they need us. That, my friends, is what it means to have a close family.

I am blessed—truly blessed. I am blessed to have a close family, and I am blessed to share with my husband the wonderful privilege of magnifying the Lord. The sacrifices seem small when I see the multiplied opportunities that started with a young dating couple who read together Psalm 34:3, "*O magnify the LORD with me, and let us exalt his name together.*" A 19-year-old Jack Schaap said to a 17-year-old Cindy Hyles, "Let's do that in our marriage, okay?"

I responded, "Okay."

And the rest has been downright wonderful! What a privilege for a family to serve and magnify the Lord from generation to generation!

Ken and Marlene Schaap   *Jack and Beverly Hyles*

3

THE VALUE
OF A MOTHER

- "I feel worthless."
- "I'm not worth anything to anyone."

These statements and statements like them may run through the mind of the average housewife and mother, especially in this age of women with college degrees and executive careers. Much of a wife's life is spent encouraging her husband to do the main job in his life—serving the Lord Jesus Christ. The hours a wife spends missing her husband while he serves the Lord may cause her to feel unimportant and worth very little.

Much of a mother's life is spent loving and training children to leave the nest. She sacrifices her time and energy to prepare her children for the person who will be number one in their life—their future spouse. When the nest is suddenly empty and the adult children are too busy, a mother may be tempted to ask, "Was my work worth anything?"

Not only are these statements far from Biblical, far from positive Christian thinking—they are also far from the truth!

In my Christian Womanhood class at Hyles-Anderson College, I teach my students the definition of self-worth.

SELF-WORTH =
THE PRICE MY CREATOR WAS WILLING
TO PAY FOR ME

I teach my students that since their Creator was willing to give His life (and His all) for them, they are worth everything. They are very valuable—indeed, priceless. And if their worth is determined by the Creator's sacrifice, then their worth or their value is unchangeable by success, failure, sin, etc.

However, a person's self-esteem can be changed. Self-esteem is the level of a person's own feelings about herself, while self-worth is the level of God's feelings about us. Allow me to give you my definition of self-esteem.

SELF-ESTEEM = DOING WHAT GOD WANTS ME TO DO

Proverbs 31:10 says, *"Who can find a virtuous woman? for her price is far above rubies."* Rubies are one of the most valuable of gemstones. They are precious stones—not one of those semi-precious ones. Proverbs 31 teaches us that the virtuous woman is not just more valuable than rubies; the Bible says she is far more valuable than rubies.

Proverbs 31 goes on to describe the very valuable woman. She is described in a way that depicts the average housewife. Her value is described in terms having to do with working with her hands around the house; food preparation; gardening; sewing; giving to the needy; wardrobe planning for her and her children; selling her wares to help the family financially; and last but not least, consistent kindness and love toward her family.

Somewhere today a godly mother will kiss her husband goodbye and send him off with words of encouragement. She will go about the duties of housewife and mother. She will change dirty diapers and rock her baby and sing lullabies. She will clean dusty corners, scrub floors, and clean toilets. She will do the things that need to be done around the house in order to free her husband to do more important things.

She will spend a good bit of her day playing dolls or trucks and winning the hearts of her children. She will perhaps play the part of a fool while telling Bible stories and singing songs to keep her children's attention. As she sacrifices her time and wonders what she'll do with her college degree, she is aware that she is preparing her children to leave the nest and live their own lives serving God, not pleasing her—and she may sometimes ask, "Is it worth it? Do the things I do have any value?"

No one will call her to the platform and applaud her work today. She will not receive an Emmy or a Golden Globe award. Her stage is her home; her pay is her grocery allowance; and her audience might be one toddler-age child. But when God decided to describe the woman of value—He described her.

When I plant my eyes upon the verses of Proverbs 31, I am reminded that God's value system is very different from the world's. In His eyes, the value of a mother is priceless.

When I think of my own mother, Beverly Hyles, and her sacrifice of her time as she reared four children, I am reminded that she is a priceless gift from God to me. When I think of my mother-in-law Marlene Schaap—what precious stories my husband tells me of her loving care for him—I am reminded that she is a valuable part of our lives.

Most of you probably won't receive any expensive jewelry from your children any time soon, but perhaps the next time you venture out to the mall, you could stop at the jewelry store. Look carefully at the largest ruby dinner ring you can find. Gaze upon a ruby tennis bracelet. Feast your eyes and your dreams upon a ruby pendant or brooch. Then when you walk away, don't say, "I can't afford that!" Don't say, "My children can't afford to buy me that." Realize how valuable you are to God, simply walk away, and say to yourself, "I'm worth more than that!"

UNIT SIX

LESSONS FOR PREACHERS' KIDS

PITFALLS OF
PREACHERS' KIDS
AND HOW TO AVOID THEM

When my husband and I were dating, we had the privilege of eating lunch with another preacher's kid. He was the son of a well-known preacher, and he was much older and wiser than I. I knew there were a lot of things I could learn from him. During our meal, he mentioned the fact that preachers' kids are notoriously suspicious. I immediately identified with what he was saying; I had noticed that tendency in my own life.

SUSPICION IS A PITFALL!

Suspicion is a trap the Devil can use in the life of the preacher's kid. Most preachers' kids at some time in their lives will see their parents used, betrayed, and criticized. It may be that some will see their parents hurt by the very people they considered their friends.

If this happens, it can really be a growing time for the pastor's children. In fact, some of the sweetest teenagers I have ever met are preachers' kids who have been through church splits with their parents. However, even the best young people can find themselves becoming suspicious after they have been through something like this with their parents. If a preacher's kid is not careful, he can become one of the most skeptical and critical people around. He can become so mistrusting that he can't get help from anyone.

One of the most amazing qualities to me about my dad was his ability to trust people. Because he had worked with such a large congregation for over 40 years, he had been "burned" time and time again. However, he was not less hesitant to trust people, nor was he less able to think good of people. His attitude has helped me in many ways.

If parents in the ministry want to help their children overcome the pitfall of suspicion, they must display trusting attitudes in their own lives. I saw this over and over again in the lives of my parents. I also think that children need to be taught from an early age that *"love thinketh no evil."* I often quote I Corinthians 13:5 in order to help myself overcome the stumbling block of suspicion. In my own struggle with suspicion, I have learned that if you let yourself become the type of person who believes the worst about people, you will become the type of person who believes anything. If you get that way, it will be very difficult to learn the qualities of friendship and loyalty that make life so much richer.

If I suspicion something evil about someone or if I suspicion that someone is trying to take advantage of me or someone I love, I immediately take that problem to the Lord. I ask the Lord to make the truth obvious to me or to the person who could be hurt. Then, I forget about it. I do not believe evil about a person because of hearsay.

On the flip side of the coin, a preacher's kid has a lot of people in his life who love him dearly just because he is the preacher's kid. I have enjoyed growing up in the same church with the same people for 47 years. I have met people of all ages who have taught me the meaning of friendship and loyalty. They have shown me by example how much these qualities can enrich lives.

The older I get, the more I focus on the people who love me. This is one of the great secrets of avoiding the pitfall of suspicion. People who love me have hurt me before and may do so again, but fellowship with God's people is a great gift from the Lord, and I praise Him for it.

CRITICISM IS A PITFALL!

Next, the preacher's kid must learn to avoid the pitfall of criticism. My parents did me two great favors when I was growing up that helped me avoid this problem.

First of all, they rarely said anything bad about anyone. When I was about 15, I remember noticing that I had never heard my dad say anything bad about anyone. The same statement can be said of my mother.

Secondly, they didn't bring the problems of the ministry home. They protected us from the trials of the ministry as much as possible.

Parents do their children a great disservice when they feel free to let their criticism be spoken and their bitterness be known in the home. If I had been brought up to be a bitter and critical person, I could not possibly have survived the trials of my parents' ministry. "Love your enemies" was lived in our home; it has been my sanity during the last few years. If there is anything I desire to teach my children, it is to love their enemies. It will get them through anything. As children of a preacher, they need not only to hear this truth but also to see it in action. I praise the Lord for the privilege of seeing it myself.

SPIRITUAL PRIDE IS A PITFALL!

We must also guard against the pitfall of spiritual pride. When I was young, there were times in my life when I was treated as if I were better than somebody else because I was the preacher's kid. My parents, however, did a lot to show me that I was no better than anyone else.

First of all, they kept me on a consistent schedule so that, believe it or not, I led a rather simple life. Our home was very organized, and our lifestyle was very simple. Our home was not at all like Grand Central Station, and considering the size of our church, that is rather amazing!

Secondly, they did not encourage talent or try to put me up in front of people a lot. They didn't pull strings to be sure I was chosen for particular groups or activities.

My parents did, however, give me a lot of praise, and they displayed a lot of confidence in my abilities. Usually, this was done privately. Therefore, it gave me a great sense of self worth without causing me to have a superior attitude.

I was always made to feel that, in order to be a good Christian, I needed to serve the Lord like everyone else. I was made to realize that I couldn't ride along on my father's coattails.

I am so grateful that I was not reared to consider myself better than others. I could not have made it through if that had been my attitude. The fact that my sense of self-worth has come first from the Lord and then from my most meaningful close relationships, instead of from an audience, has been my mainstay.

BUSYNESS IS A PITFALL!

Last of all, we must avoid the pitfall of busyness. The criticism about my dad that was the most difficult for me to bear was that he didn't spend time with us when we were children. First of all, how could anyone who didn't grow up in our home possibly know?

Of course, there were times when our dad wasn't around when we wished he could have been, but I remember my dad as never being too busy for his children. When my dad got home from church, he would stay up for hours talking to his family regardless of how late it was. He never seemed tired or burdened, and of course, his children never knew that he was. I don't know of any of my friends whose dads stayed up until midnight talking with them around the kitchen table. My dad never seemed too busy for me; he was a lot of fun and always seemed to be happy.

My mom was always there for us, too. As I mentioned earlier, she kept us on a very strict and simple schedule. In order to keep us on that schedule, she often excused herself from activities early so that she could be at home when we got in from school. We were a priority in her life, and she was there for us.

Now my husband and I are very busy in the ministry, and we are challenged to avoid the pitfall of being too busy for our very important children. I praise the Lord for the example set by his parents and mine.

PREACHERS' KIDS HAVE A RICH LIFE!

These four areas stand out in my mind as possible pitfalls for the preacher's kid. With the Lord's help, these things have actually been turned into assets for me in many ways. Being a preacher's kid is a rich life—a perfect mixture of the bitter and the sweet. I wouldn't trade my life for anyone else's. I praise the Lord for my parents and the special calling God gave them.

UNIT SEVEN

LOSING A CHILD

1

THOU HAST VISITED ME IN THE NIGHT

This chapter is lovingly dedicated to all women who have ever lost a child.

On February 20, 2004, over a lunch date, our daughter Jaclynn told me that my husband and I were going to be grandparents for the first time. I was ecstatic! I wrote down the date of February 20 in my Bible next to Ruth 4:15: *"And he shall be unto thee a restorer of thy life, and a nourisher of thine old age…"* speaking of the grandson of Naomi.

Todd and Jaclynn asked my husband and me to wait a month to announce it, which we gladly did. On March 16, I spilled the beans at the ladies' sessions of Pastors' School. I must admit that the theme of Pastors' School that year, "Reaching the Next Generation," meant extra much to me.

For two months our family laughed and giggled together about the coming baby. For two months I prayed daily for the coming baby. For several weeks Jaclynn struggled with the dreaded morning sickness!

On April 21, 2004, Jaclynn had a doctor's appointment. She invited me to go with her. In mother/daughter fashion, we giggled all the way. I ate lunch in the waiting room and teased that it looked like I was the one who was expecting a baby!

Jaclynn went into the doctor's office alone and came out with a dif-

ferent attitude. She had an ultrasound, and no baby could be found. We
were sent to the hospital for another ultrasound, and my husband and
Todd came to be with us. At first we were told that Jaclynn had a tumor,
and we were very concerned about her.

On Thursday we learned that there was not a tumor but that
Jaclynn had indeed miscarried. The plan was for Jaclynn to enter the
hospital the following Sunday afternoon and for labor to be induced on
Sunday evening.

I hurt deeply for Jaclynn and Todd and cried for two days…

Jaclynn went home from the hospital on Monday evening, April 26,
and her six-day ordeal was finally ended. But, of course, her grief was
just beginning.

There is an inclination of the flesh to question why God allows such
things to happen and to feel that He has turned His hand of blessing
from us. I had prayed every day that Jaclynn would not miscarry and
that she would bring forth a healthy baby. I know better than to pay any
attention to my feelings and thoughts during such times, but the feelings and thoughts were there.

On the morning after we learned of Jaclynn's miscarriage, I read the
following verse in my daily Bible reading: Psalm 17:3a, *"Thou hast proved
mine heart; thou hast visited me in the night.…"* In the margin of my John
R. Rice Reference Bible, the words, *"thou hast visited me in the night,"* are
interpreted to mean "thou hast come to deal with me personally." I felt
like that was my answer from the Lord to my quiet questioning, "Are you
mad at us, God?" God is not angry with us when He allows heartache
in our lives. Sometimes He just wants to "deal with us personally," or as
my husband would say, "God sometimes 'gets in our face' " because He
wants to show us how much He loves us.

I want to learn from every heartache what God wants me to learn.
Sometimes it may be that He wants to correct something in my life, but
that is okay with me. As long as God is dealing with me personally, I
know that I am going to be fine—even if that dealing hurts sometimes.
The following are some other things I learned from our daughter's miscarriage. These are some ways God dealt with me personally through
this trial.

1. **God showed me that I have a strong daughter who walks with God.** Jaclynn always had a great walk with God when she lived at home. Of course, now that she lives elsewhere, I cannot know her walk with God as I once did. Yet it was very clear to me as I watched Jaclynn's suffering that she still has a great relationship with her God. Though she hurt deeply, her strength was great!

2. **God showed me that I have a great son-in-law.** I was so comforted by the way I saw Todd treat Jaclynn during their trial. It was a calming experience to watch Todd's and Jaclynn's marriage through their suffering. There was a joy and contentment between them that can only come to two people who really love and enjoy each other.

3. **God gave me another group of people whom I can comfort.** I could not feel sorry for our daughter during her loss without thinking of the many people who have lost babies. I thought of Rafael and Kelly Cowling Cervantes who have lost three children—baby Sara at eight months old, baby Scott when he was 12 days old, and baby Susanna who was stillborn.

I have visited and comforted those who have lost babies. I saw some of those faces of those mothers who had miscarried as I went through it with our daughter, and I wished that I had known then what I know now.

4. **God reminded me again of what a precious treasure the Bible is to our family.** My husband shared with me the verse that he read in his Bible reading the next morning. Psalm 113:9, *"He maketh the barren woman to keep house, and to be a joyful mother of children. Praise ye the LORD."*

Jaclynn shared with me the verse that she read in her Bible reading that week: Psalm 23:4, *"Yea, though I walk through the valley of the shadow of death, I will fear no evil: for thou art with me; thy rod and thy staff they comfort me."*

The grandchild we never knew was already the owner of a baby book, a playpen, and a video entitled, "The Little Engine That Could." This grandma had grand plans of helping convince this child that he could do ANYTHING! The grandchild we never knew was deeply loved and prayed for. I couldn't believe how much I had to change my prayer list after we discovered he was in Heaven. This grandchild we never knew was greatly anticipated. I can only begin to understand how much more loss Todd and Jaclynn felt over their child they never knew.

Yet this grandchild we never knew has taught me some lessons.

1.   He has reminded me of the wonderful people that I have been allowed to have in my life—a strong and loving husband, sweet children, and comforting church members whom I have been privileged to know. All are great blessings from the Lord.

2.   Our grandchild we never knew has reminded me how many hurting people need my love.

3.   Most of all, the grandchild we never knew has reminded me that no matter where we are—on earth or in Heaven—as long as God is dealing with us personally, we are blessed and we are safe.

II Samuel 12:23b, *"I shall go to him, but he shall not return to me."* We will never forget and—praise the Lord!—someday we will meet the grandchild we never knew.

2

LESSONS ON CHILD REARING FROM THE LIVES OF JOCHEBED AND HANNAH

I Samuel 1:1-28; Exodus 2:1-10

The following lessons are taken from the life of Jochebed, who was the mother of Moses, and Hannah, who was the mother of Samuel.

1. **It takes desire to rear a good child.** *"And she was in bitterness of soul, and prayed unto the LORD, and wept sore."* (I Samuel 1:10) Hannah really wanted a child. She prayed in agony that God would give her one. We show our children how much they were wanted by spending time with them and by giving them priority in our lives.

It is easy to want a child when you are childless, but how about when they are keeping you up all night with colic or how about when they are rebellious teenagers. Always make your children feel cherished and wanted.

2. **It takes fervent prayer to rear a good child.** *"And she vowed a vow, and said, O LORD of hosts, if thou wilt indeed look on the affliction of thine handmaid, and remember me, and not forget thine handmaid, but wilt give unto thine handmaid a man child, then I will give him unto the LORD all the days of his life, and there shall no razor come upon his head."* (I Samuel 1:11) Again, Hannah begged God for Samuel.

231

3.   **In order to rear a good child, one must see his higher good.** Hannah showed her vision for her son Samuel by giving him to God to serve and to live with Eli in the temple.

Jochebed showed her vision for her son Moses by placing him in an ark of bulrushes and leaving him in the hands of the Lord so that he might be saved from being killed by Pharaoh's army. Exodus 2:2, 3 says, *"And the woman conceived, and bare a son: and when she saw him that he was a goodly child, she hid him three months. And when she could not longer hide him, she took for him an ark of bulrushes, and daubed it with slime and with pitch, and put the child therein; and she laid it in the flags by the river's brink."*

4.   **It takes faith and courage to rear a good child.** It took faith for Jochebed to carry her child to full term when she knew the king's edict said he would be killed. It took faith for Jochebed to hide Moses in her home for three months. It took faith to prepare a boat and to place baby Moses in the river. It took faith to trust Moses to the Lord's care while he was being reared as the son of Pharoah's daughter.

A mother should learn to overcome her fears so as not to pass them on to her children. Practice saying to your children, "Everything is going to be all right." This is something my husband said frequently to our children when they were growing up. Let your children enjoy their childhood under the umbrella of your faith.

The words *"…saw him that he was a goodly child"* means that Jochebed had faith to believe that God had a purpose for Moses' life. Jochebed must have had a close walk with God to see that Moses was a goodly child.

5.   **It takes creativity to rear a good child.** Jochebed came up with a creative way, under the Lord's direction, to save her son. Her creativity passed on to her daughter Miriam. Miriam creatively offered to find a nurse for Moses. *"Then said his sister to Pharaoh's daughter, Shall I go and call to thee a nurse of the Hebrew women, that she may nurse the child for thee? And Pharaoh's daughter said to her, Go. And the maid went and called the child's mother. And Pharaoh's daughter said unto her, Take this child away, and nurse it for me, and I will give thee thy wages. And the woman took the child, and nursed it."* (Exodus 2:7-9)

6.   **It takes love for one's spouse to rear a good child.** The Bible

teaches that Elkanah favored his wife Hannah. Hannah was a good wife. This relationship probably helped Hannah to let go of her son as she left him at the temple. *"But unto Hannah he gave a worthy portion; for he loved Hannah: but the LORD had shut up her womb."* (I Samuel 1:5)

   7.   **In order to rear a good child, a mother cannot make herself the issue.** I can hardly imagine placing my baby boy in a tiny boat and sending him floating down the Nile River. As the children's song says, "I wonder who would come—a princess or a hungry crocodile."

   But what is even harder for me to imagine is watching some unsaved woman who worshiped heathen gods rearing my child as her son and my standing by pretending to be his nurse. Sure, Jochebed was excited the child was going to live—at first, but at some point she must have wanted to spill the beans about Moses' identity. At some point, I believe I would have said, "HE'S **MY** SON!" (Sounds like dialogue from the mouth of a jealous mother-in-law.) But Jochebed never breathed a word. I wonder if the humility that Jochebed displayed in denying her rights of motherhood was what influenced her son Moses to be, as he was called by God, "the meekest man in all the earth." Numbers 12:3 says, *"(Now the man Moses was very meek, above all the men which were upon the face of the earth.)"* Pride and arrogance would certainly have hindered Moses from fulfilling his purpose in life of freeing and leading the children of Israel.

   A little boy adores his mother. One of my favorite pictures of me and Kenny is one where I am holding him on my lap when he is about three years old. Kenny is sucking his thumb, and I am smiling and thinking about how much fun it is to be the mother of a three-year-old boy. It is written all over my face in the photograph, and I remember it like it was yesterday. As Kenny grew older, he began to instead adore his father—a normal and even necessary change for a little boy. I remember Kenny proclaiming to his sister, "I look like Dad, and you look like Mom." To which Jaclynn argued, "No, I look like Dad, and you look like Mom!" Such conversations can tempt one toward having an inferiority complex!

   At 16 years of age, Kenny began to notice the girl that he says is the prettiest and the best in the world to him. (I think I held that title once!) Her name is Candace. After Kenny dated her for over four years, on December 17, 2005, she became his wife. When Candace married Kenny, I wrote a letter and told her that I was giving Kenny to her freely and wholly. I was training him for her to begin with. He was not really mine.

But there is one more thing that takes my mother rights away from me—just like Jochebed and Hannah lost theirs—and that is the will of God. The will of God for Kenny will not be a boat made of bulrushes or living in the temple, but it is just as real and sacred. And it just as much relinquishes my mother rights on Kenny.

I know I brought him into the world; the labor was painful; I loved him; I cared for him for 21 years, but I relinquish my mother rights because that is what it takes to rear a good child. And a son will appreciate and respect a mother who doesn't make herself the issue.

8.   **It takes vision to rear a good child.** We should have a vision for our child, but we should not have a plan. Jochebed had a vision for Moses. She "saw" he was a "proper child." Her vision caused Jochebed to put Moses in the river, but Jochebed did not have a plan. I'm sure if she had, it would not have been for Moses to have been reared by Pharaoh's daughter. It is okay to have a plan for rearing our children, but we must let God make the plans for their life's calling and so forth.

I believe a Biblical vision for a son is for him to do God's will. A Biblical vision for a daughter is for her to be a good wife to the person God has for her to marry. These were my visions as I reared Kenny and Jaclynn, and these visions motivated me to give my best in rearing them—especially at times when it was difficult.

There are three things that hinder us from having a proper vision for our children:

A.   Selfishness. Many parents want their children to make them happy in their adult lives. A young child who is reared properly brings much joy to his parents. Jaclynn and Kenny have brought much joy to my husband and to me. I teased them as they got older, "If you were going to grow up and move out, you should not have been so nice to me." There is a little bit of truth to that teasing. It is hard to be unselfish with children who have been such a joy. But I did not rear our children for selfish reasons. I reared Kenny to do God's will, and I reared Jaclynn to be a good wife to Todd Weber. Both children still bring me much joy. But at seasons when I rarely see them, I remind myself that they were not made to make me happy, and I should not complain when their schedules cause them to see me less than I desire. Also, if God were to call them to serve Him miles away, I want to be happy for them—even if it is painful for me. I am happy if Kenny is doing God's will and if Jaclynn is helping her husband to do God's will.

B. *A competitive spirit.* When we rear our children with a vision for them to be better than other children, we sometimes are tempted to plan their lives rather than just to have a vision for God's will. It matters not to me if my friends' children do something greater, humanly speaking, than mine do. I just want Kenny to do God's will and Jaclynn to help Todd to do God's will.

C. *Not being on the same page with their father.* I have often stated that adaptability is a woman's greatest ability. This is true in child rearing. I had a plan about how to rear our children, and my husband had a plan. In order to be both a good wife and mother, it was my job to adapt to my husband's plan. Now that Kenny is an adult, I must adapt to God's plan and vision for him. Now that Jaclynn is an adult, I must adapt to Todd's plans for Jaclynn. It is up to Kenny to find God's will for his life, and it is up to Todd to find God's will for Jaclynn. My job is to pray that they will find God's will.

9. It takes commitment to rear a good child. It took commitment for Hannah to leave that much-prayed-for toddler at the temple and to say, "I'll see you in a year." It took commitment to float that little boat down the Nile and to bite the lip as another woman took Jochebed's place as mother. It took commitment to rear a great prophet Samuel, but without that commitment, would we even know of Hannah and Samuel?

It took commitment to rear Moses as a great deliverer of a great nation, but without that commitment, would we even know of Jochebed and Moses? Would we know the greatness of God as we have discovered it through the miracles wrought through Moses' ministry.

It takes commitment to rear a child to serve the Lord, but without that commitment, what is the purpose of rearing children anyway?

WHAT IT TAKES TO LOSE A CHILD

Psalm 106:24-27 gives a contrasting view of how some other Jewish women from the Old Testament lost their children. *"Yea, they despised the pleasant land, they believed not his word: But murmured in their tents, and hearkened not unto the voice of the LORD. Therefore he lifted up his hand against them, to overthrow them in the wilderness: To overthrow their seed also among the nations, and to scatter them in the lands."* Many of the Jewish mothers lost their children to heathen nations. Why?

A. They despised God's will for their lives. The word *despise* means "belittle." God's will was for them to leave Egypt and to enter the Promised Land, but some despised and mocked this idea. Mothers who make fun of those who serve the Lord will lose their children to the heathen.

B. They did not have faith in God. They didn't believe God's Word. In order to rear a good child, a mother needs to stay in the Bible and to trust its words. She needs to constantly strengthen her faith, believing that God will bless her efforts to rear a child to serve the Lord and not for her own pleasure.

C. They complained in their houses. Mothers who are often found complaining about God's will and how hard they have it will lose their children. Children need to see their parents serving the Lord with gladness.

D. They did not listen to God's voice. A wise mother should listen to and obey the voice of God, especially in the areas of submission to her husband and in child rearing.

Two mothers living under adverse circumstances reared sons who brought honor to their names, while others among the children of Israel reared children who were lost to heathen nations. What was the difference? Many mothers lived for self, but two women—Jochebed and Hannah—did not make themselves the issue.

Unit Eight

Lessons From the Previous Generation

.

1

Heirlooms From My Parents

I n the same year that I turned the big 3-0, my parents, Dr. and Mrs. Jack Hyles, celebrated the thirtieth year of their long, successful pastorate at First Baptist Church of Hammond, Indiana. In November 1959 during their first year in Hammond, I entered the world as the fourth child (or as my parents would say "the baby") of the Hyles family. I honestly believe God put me in this particular family because He knew how stubborn I was going to be. Whatever the reason, it has a been a great privilege.

As I have thought back over my life, I realized that my parents handed me something valuable that makes life only seem richer as the decades pass and more secure as the trials come.

I'm not speaking of anything material. Though I've enjoyed some wonderful shopping trips with both my mom and dad, they've not lavished expensive gifts on me. Neither do they claim any investment program from which I might inherit a small fortune. No, the things they've given go beyond that. They are not material things and are inexpensive and yet, priceless.

My parents taught me some lessons through their words and example. These lessons have made my years very happy ones, and I believe the remaining years I have can be as happy because these truths can still be with me.

I could never in one chapter or in one book or in an entire library write all the things I have learned from my parents, but please allow me the privilege of passing on four of the most important truths I have been taught and given. I call them my heirlooms.

1. God is GOOD. *"I know, O LORD, that thy judgments are right, and that thou in faithfulness hast afflicted me."* (Psalm 119:75) That seems like an easy enough lesson to teach, but it is not. However, my parents have successfully taught through their actions that God is always good. I have never seen either one of my parents question God when trials came into their lives. They have always pointed me to the fact that God is in control of our lives.

In my first decade of being an adult, I came across many people who had left God behind because He had disappointed them. If ever two people could have had a right to question God, it would have been my parents. They gave their all in the battle for Christ and saw much disappointment, yet I never saw their faith waver. It looked easy at sixteen, but I now know it has been difficult. Still, I cling to this faith and struggle to pass it on to my own two children. My children deserve the privileges I have had.

2. God is LOVE. At approximately 16 years of age, when driving home from church one Sunday night with my dad, it dawned on me that I had never heard my dad say anything bad about anyone. I really believe it was that night that I decided I wanted his type of Christianity. John 13:35 says, *"By this shall all men know that ye are my disciples, if ye have love one to another."* I think some children do not follow their parents' faith because they haven't seen Christ's love in their parents' lives.

I have witnessed God's love in my parents' lives, and I want that kind of love in my own life. I don't know what it feels like to be bitter. I do know what it feels like to love my enemies and my parents' enemies. It is one of the greatest feelings ever. I hope I can "pass it on" to my children. They deserve the privileges I've had.

3. God is REAL. As you can see, all of the lessons I am sharing with you are about God. My parents have always pointed others to the Lord—not themselves. Yet they have done it in a fun and practical way. My dad has always said one of the most important steps in rearing children is to make God practical in their lives. My parents made God practical in our home as we learned much about Him through laughter and silliness.

Because we are not perfect, some have passed judgment on my parents and the sacrifices they have made in the ministry (usually people who know nothing about what they're saying). I just happen to be an expert witness in this matter, and let me say that my parents were always there when we needed them as children.

They were there teaching about God in a practical way. My dad sometimes used practical and humorous methods in teaching others about God at First Baptist Church and Hyles-Anderson College. I have found this method to make God only more real and His Word more profound. I hope I can make God real for our children's lives. They deserve the privileges I've had.

4.   God is FIRST. *"But seek ye first the kingdom of God, and his righteousness; and all these things shall be added unto you."* (Matthew 6:33) Yes, the ministry and the will of God have been first in my parents' lives, and they have given basically everything for God's will. I think it is something of which they should be proud.

Money has never been an issue in their lives. Surely they argued sometimes over money—surely they fretted—but I never knew it. Again, this is something I took for granted until I became a parent. I now realize that money leads people away from the ministry and discourages children from ever wanting to follow in "full-time Christian work." If a parent does not make money an issue in the home, it is because of a lot of hard work. My parents' philosophy about money is one I want.

As I reminisce about my heirlooms from my parents, I realize how truly blessed I am for this intangible inheritance that has made my life only seem richer. How I thank them for these priceless truths they diligently taught me.

2

THEY LOVED ME ENOUGH TO CORRECT ME

The following verses helped me to accept correction and teaching as I was growing up.

"Blessed is the man whom thou chastenest, O LORD, and teachest him out of thy law." (Psalm 94:12)

"Chasten thy son while there is hope, and let not thy soul spare for his crying." (Proverbs 19:18)

"For whom the Lord loveth he chasteneth, and scourgeth every son whom he receiveth." (Hebrews 12:6)

"Now no chastening for the present seemeth to be joyous, but grievous; nevertheless afterward it yieldeth the peaceable fruit of righteousness unto them which are exercised thereby." (Hebrew 12:11)

"As many as I love, I rebuke and chasten: be zealous therefore, and repent." (Revelation 3:19)

MY PARENTS LOVED ME ENOUGH TO:
- Make me stay awake during family altar.
- Be honest with me when discussing areas where I needed improvement.
- Make me quit hanging around with a very good friend who was in sin.

- Make me clean my room.
- Make me spend hours practicing good manners.
- Not allow me to get too involved with public school friends.
- Make me come home early from dates.
- Never allow me to date alone in cars.
- Make me go to all the church-oriented activities.
- Spank me.
- Make me spend time alone to think what I had done wrong.
- Take me to church when I was first born.
- Make me sit on the front row when I was a child.
- Make me stay awake in church.
- Not allow me to play around with toys in church.
- Make me obey them.
- Not allow me to touch certain things in the house.
- Make me eat foods I didn't like.
- Make me have proper table manners even when eating with the family.
- Make me chew with my mouth closed at all times.
- Make me stay at the table until the whole family was done eating.
- Make me thank my mother for every meal.
- Make me ask to be excused before leaving the table after eating.
- Make me help to set the table.
- Make me help to clear the table.
- Make me memorize Scripture.
- Make me read the Bible.
- Make me read my dad's book *Blue Denim and Lace*.
- Not allow me to wear pants.
- Not allow me to attend movies.
- Not allow me to go mixed swimming.
- Not allow me to wear short skirts.
- Not allow me to listen to rock music.
- Not allow me to watch movies on television.
- Not allow me to watch soap operas.

- Not allow me to read *Mad Magazine*.
- Lecture me on being a good wife.
- Not allow me to read pornographic literature.
- Not allow me to watch or listen to cigarette commercials.
- Not allow me to watch or listen to beer commercials.
- Warn me about things even if it scared me so I would be aware of certain dangers.
- Not let me wear too much makeup.
- Make me wear modest-fitting clothes.
- Be consistent in discipline.
- Not let me idolize movie stars.
- Not let me be worldly.
- Shelter me.
- Keep me ignorant in certain matters.
- Not let me hate anyone.
- Rebuke me when I mentioned hating anyone.
- Teach me not to be bitter against anyone or anything.
- Not let me do seemingly harmless things that other Christian teenagers were allowed to do.
- Spend hours teaching me what real happiness was when I would rather have been doing something else.
- Not allow me to be in the limelight when I wanted to be.
- Make me achieve on my own.
- Make me like other kids and not let me be different or special because of who I was.
- Expect my respect for them.
- Expect me to spoil them.
- Make me be good to my sisters and brother.
- Make me be good to my grandmother.
- Make me go to bed on time.
- Give me the security of hearing "no."

3

WHAT MY PARENTS DID RIGHT

I read one day about a man who had a lamppost near his house. It was at this lamppost where he left his burdens in an imaginary and yet very real sort of a way. He left them there so that he could be cheerful when he arrived home to see his family. Ever since I read that story, I have wondered where my dad's lamppost was.

One of the many things that dad did right was that he never brought his problems home to his family. We were unaware of many of the problems that occurred in his ministry during our growing up years. I believe Dad kept his problems from us because he believed that everyone has a right to be a child for a while. Dad definitely afforded us that privilege.

Dad had a sense of humor that made him the enthusiasm of our home. I remember a lot of crazy things he did that he probably wished I would forget. I recall a night when he decided to take several of my sister's and my large stuffed animals and put them around the table in the kitchen. Dad then set the table and made it look as if our animals were eating breakfast. His purpose was not only to entertain his onlooking daughters, but also to startle my mother when she came to fix breakfast the next morning. The story seems silly as I write about it now, but I remember the fun we had that night, and I remember how well Dad seemed to relate with us when he played one of his "teenage" pranks. I have fond memories of Dad's pulling our sleds down the street in front of our home in Munster, Indiana. I recall his loud and jovial methods of waking us up in the morning, whether it was in our bedroom or at the breakfast table.

As a child, I always took for granted Dad's joviality. My child's mind figured that Dad did all those things just because he wanted to have fun. As I have practiced being a parent myself, I realize that it takes much discipline and love to be as jovial as Dad was when you are carrying the burdens of the ministry. I tried to discipline myself to protect my children from as much negative news as possible so that they might have the privilege to enjoy their childhood as I did.

Dad was a tremendous communicator. He often asked our advice about what tie he should wear with a particular suit, what type of punishment he should give us in regards to a certain infraction of the rules, etc. When I was with Dad, I always had the feeling that he wanted to be with me. Perhaps that is what made Dad the most special to me. I always had the feeling that he not only loved me, but I felt that he liked me very much. My most poignant recollection of Dad's communication skills is our talks around the kitchen table late at night.

Almost every night that my dad was in town, we would sit around the kitchen table until late at night discussing life. As much as my dad loved humor, he loved to philosophize, and he philosophized with his children as if they were adults. Dad valued good communication between parent and child more than he valued a good night's rest. Though my own children had a set bedtime, I often allowed them to stay up a little later if it meant some individual time with their dad or me. I realized from my own experience that a child can get along without sleep better than he can get along without personal and positive attention from Mom and/or Dad.

People have often thanked me for giving up my dad to help save America, but I have never felt that I gave up my dad. Many kids had dads who went to their basketball games when my dad was out of town. However, I knew a lot of kids whose dads were **in town**, and yet their dad never came to the games either. I didn't know any kids who I felt had as good communication with their dad as I did. Through this communication, I became very close to my dad, and there were many wrong things that I wanted to do when I was a teenager that I did not do because I did not want to disappoint my dad.

Dad communicated to me in verbal and non-verbal ways that he was putting my interests before his own, and I never got the impression that he was trying to rear me to be a good girl so that I would enhance his reputation as a preacher. This was very important to me. I probably made more mistakes in high school than my other three siblings put together, and Dad never mentioned his reputation or being embarrassed one time. Neither did my mom for that matter.

When I was 15 years old, I heard through the grapevine that one of the faculty members of Hammond Baptist High School had been seriously disciplined. While riding home with my dad one Sunday night after church, I decided to take advantage of my preacher's kid's position and try to find out what happened. My dad refused to give me any of the facts, and I realized something that night that startled me. I remember clearly that was the night I decided that I would like to be the same type of Christian my dad was. I decided that my dad was for real. My dad never communicated any bitterness about the people who hurt him in the ministry. I have never really struggled with bitterness myself, and I realize I owe a lot to my dad for that.

Because of my dad's strong preaching on standards, etc. people sometimes viewed my dad as mean and unloving. I saw the other side of Dad. In fact, I never remember his raising his voice in our home. I'm not sure Dad would appreciate my saying so, but to me he was as gentle as a lamb.

Both my mom and dad made God very real to me. God was never a spooky Being Who lived far away somewhere, but rather, I felt that He was comfortable living right in our home. He seemed to fit well into every part of our lives, not just into our church going on Sundays. I think my parents' sense of humor and consistency as Christians made this possible.

As much as my preacher dad was the enthusiasm and the zeal of our home, my beautiful and graceful mother was the quiet, steady and sensitive spirit of our home. Each parent had a very intricate and unique part in my life. My mother taught me to love routine, organization, and schedule because she loved all those. My mother found as much creative challenge in a quiet day of homemaking as my dad found in his most fiery sermon. My mother's enjoyment of little things is something that I best remember about her. She could squeeze a lot of joy out of a simple cup of coffee and a good book. It was her enjoyment of schedule and routine that provided me with the security that a girl with one parent who traveled a lot might not have had. A hearty breakfast was ready promptly at the same time each morning, and dinner was served at exactly 5:00. My mother also gave me a love for neatness by her example. Our home was always in beautiful order. I think this type of organization also enhanced my security as a child.

My mother's love for routine and for her Lord showed in the fact that she was usually reading her Bible at the kitchen table when I left to go to school each morning. That memory is a wonderful part of my heritage.

My mother's sensitive spirit often brought her to my bedroom to apologize if she felt she had mishandled me or my brother or my sisters in any way. I always appreciated her willingness to be open about her humanity. I always felt that my mother tried to live the sermons that my dad preached. I often noticed that she would find a way to indoctrinate something into our lives that had been said in my dad's sermon the previous week.

The thing that I needed the most in my mother was the thing that she was best able to give, that is, her quiet, steady presence. Mrs. Fay Dodson, a leader of one of the soul-winning ministries at First Baptist Church, mentioned to me a couple of years ago that my mom had excused herself from an important meeting so that she could be home when her kids got home from school. I believe that I was 30 years old when Fay shared this with me, but tears still came to my eyes. I appreciate the fact that Mom took time to be a mom.

When I was young, it seemed that I would live in Mom and Dad's house forever. Yet the years sped by quickly, and my time to be really "mothered" was relatively short. My mother has become a speaker, an author, an artist and many other things since her kids have left the "nest." The opportunities have been many. Yet she will never have another opportunity to rear me. I am thankful that she was a "keeper at home" when I was growing up.

When I was 16 years old, my mom sent word to me one Wednesday afternoon that she might not be able to pick me up after school because she had a meeting to attend. Mom suggested that I ride home in a particular car pool in which I had ridden home many times before. As it turned out, my mom was waiting for me when I got out of school just as she had been many times before. My car pool friends were in a serious accident, and my best pal Sharon was nearly killed. I often wonder if Mom's being there saved my life that particular day, but I am sure that her quiet, steady presence saved my life in other ways time and time again.

I am grateful to both of my parents for helping me find my husband. It was my mom who woke me up in the early morning hours to suggest that I date a man named Jack Schaap. She had never done anything like this before. It was my dad who walked into my bedroom one day and announced that Jack Schaap loved me and that I was to be very careful how I treated him from that day forward. Both of my parents have not only helped me to make the most important decisions of my life, but they have loved me unconditionally, and they have loved my brother, my sisters, and me fairly. They have gone to great lengths to be sure that we were all treated equally.

Lastly, my parents did right in never changing or quitting. While my parents' personalities are opposite in some respect, I always felt that both understood the greatness of God and His will for their lives. I sensed their commitment to that will. My prayer is that I would continue serving the Lord even if my parents ever did change or quit. Yet, that is something that I have never had to face. My father served the Lord until He went to Heaven. My mother has grown stronger in her commitment to Christ as she has grown older.

4

WHAT I LEARNED FROM MY DAD AND MY MOM

ON LEADERSHIP

I remember my dad taking me out to eat one day and my asking him to take me to a different restaurant than the one he suggested. I remember my dad acting slightly irritated and going ahead and taking me to the restaurant he had chosen. I also recall that the next time we went out to eat, Dad took me to the restaurant about which I had voiced a preference. From this experience, I learned the following lessons on leadership.

1. Leadership studies the needs of its followers.
2. Leadership tries to meet those needs.
3. Leadership studies the desires of its followers.
4. Leadership tries to meet those desires.
5. Leadership asks questions but not at the time the decision is being made.
6. Leadership is willing to lead. It will make the decision at the time it needs to be made.
7. Leadership takes itself out of the issue and does what is best for the followers.
8. Leadership doesn't whine.
9. Leadership uses these methods to win both the respect and the heart of its followers.
10. Leadership plans for its followers.

11.　Leadership is willing to go against the desires of its followers if that is what is best for the followers.

I am thankful that my dad had a plan when he took me on a date. I am also grateful that he followed his plan, even if I expressed another desire. It taught me something about followship and leadership. A good parent will plan things that meet the needs and desires of his children.

A good father will teach his children (especially his daughters) submission by planning things himself and sticking to the plan. Then he can use previously mentioned desires and needs to formulate future plans. There are two types of parents that contrast with these philosophies.

A.　The "Whatever" Parent. So many fathers fail in leadership because they refuse to lead their wives and children in the little decisions as well as the big decisions. A wife or children will enjoy getting their way for a while, but they will quickly tire of a leader who refuses to plan for them.

B.　The Self-Serving Parent. The self-serving parent ignores the needs and the desires of his children and deems them unimportant. Any planning on the part of this type of parent revolves mainly around the needs and desires of the parent. In worst case scenario, this type of parent is an abusive parent.

My dad used to come home late at night and stay up an hour just talking and goofing off with his family. As the pastor of a mega church, he must have been exhausted, but he never acted exhausted. My dad once bought me a very trendy dress that he told me he hated—because I liked it. My dad once cried very hard for a heartache that we both faced. He said his tears were not for him though; they were for me.

My dad dressed up as a limousine driver and drove me and several friends to downtown Chicago for my sixteenth birthday at a fancy restaurant. My dad sat in the lobby and read the paper while my friends and I had a party and ate dinner.

My dad flew my sister Linda and me and one friend each to one of his speaking engagements. He planned a party that took place on the private airplane.

All of these are examples of ways my dad planned for his children, according to their desire, and took himself out of the center of the issue.

Yet my dad was not hesitant to give us strict standards. We had an 11:00 p.m. curfew, and we were punished if we broke it. We were not allowed to watch certain television programs. We were required to dress a certain way. All of these things not only helped me to learn how to follow, but also helped me to learn about both the strength and beauty of leadership.

ON PUNISHMENT

1. They didn't raise their voice.
2. They waited before they spanked.
3. They followed the same ritual for spanking.
4. They hated that they had to punish.
5. They punished their children anyway, because it was best.
6. They clearly explained the punishment.
7. They prayed after punishment.
8. They expressed affection after punishment.
9. They stood with authority.
10. They asked for advice in making new rules.

One time Dad had planned to take our family to the circus. He began to question if he should. His secretary, Erma McKinney, had expressed that her family did not go to the circus because of the way the women were immodestly dressed.

Dad came home and said, "I promised you could go to the circus tonight, so I will take you." He told me and my brother and sisters what Mrs. McKinney had said. He allowed us to choose whether to go to the circus or to the park and McDonald's. We chose the latter to please him, but I believe he was wise in offering to keep his word and in allowing us to choose.

When I was 17, I came home late from church on a Sunday night because I had gone to Taco Bell with some friends. I was late for our 11:00 p.m. curfew. Dad asked me how I thought I should be punished. I suggested some type of grounding. Dad followed my advice.

ABOUT SCHEDULE

1. They got up at the same time each morning. They rarely slept in.
2. They got dressed first thing each morning.
3. They ate breakfast with their family each morning.
4. Dad left for work at the same time each morning.
5. Dad came home for dinner each night he was in town.
6. Mom served dinner at the same time each evening.
7. Dad would visit late into the night with his family each evening he was in town.
8. Dad had a weekly date with each child.
9. Mom and Dad had a family night when we usually went out to eat.
10. Dad helped dress the small children on Sundays.
11. Dad helped with the dishes on Sundays and holidays.
12. Dad went out of town the same days each trip.

All of these disciplines brought a sense of rhythm to our family. They also made me feel very loved and stable, in spite of the fact that our parents were very busy.

5

WHAT I LEARNED ON MY LAST NIGHT WITH MY DAD

My father's heart surgery began on Monday morning, February 5, 2001. He had been in the hospital for a week, and my mom had almost never left his side. However, on Sunday evening, February 4, Dad asked my mom to go home and get some rest. Both of my parents knew it would be a long, hard day of waiting the next day. I was elected to be the one to miss Sunday evening church and to be with my dad at the hospital. Dad never became conscious after his surgery the next day, and he went to Heaven the morning after. The following are some lessons I learned on my last night with my dad.

1. **Allow people to wait on you.** Not long after I arrived in Dad's room, he asked me to help him eat his supper. It was my pleasure and privilege to feed Dad a steak dinner. Several times as I fed Dad, he asked me to adjust his pillows. His heart condition gave him severe back pain.

Dad had everything that a man could want. The wonderful people of our church spoiled him and loved him. As a preacher's kid, I often felt the need to know I could do something for Dad that no one else could. My father was very good at making me feel needed. I really loved feeding my dad his steak and mashed potatoes. Like his daughter, Dad loved to eat, even up until the end of his journey on earth. Even as I was adjusting his pillows and feeding him dinner, I wondered if Dad really needed the help, or if he was just trying to make me feel needed. It was so like Dad to make others feel that he needed their help.

2. **Never lose your sense of humor.** At one point, I was feeding Dad his small bites of steak too quickly. (I would not make a very good nurse, I'm afraid.) Dad laughed and said, "Please don't choke me to death before my heart surgery." We both laughed. I have missed Dad every day since he went to Heaven. I think of him more often, instead of less. But I am happy. One of the things that has sustained me has been the sense of humor that I learned from my father.

3. **Be appreciative of what people do for you.** Dad had a favorite nurse named John. He was the last person Dad saw on this earth. He took Dad into surgery. When John came into the room that Sunday evening, Dad asked, "John, did you know my daughter wrote a book about me? She wrote my biography; it's over 500 pages long."

How I loved the man lying in that hospital bed! I remember thinking how often Dad bragged on me to others. His indirect praise always reached my heart and made me feel special.

That night my dad asked me to be sure that John got a copy of his biography. John visited our church and was given a biography. Several months later, on my forty-third birthday, I was able to lead John to the Lord in his home.

4. **Don't leave things unsaid.** My father was a very loving person. I never left his presence without his hugging me, kissing me on the cheek, and telling me he loved me. Occasionally, he told me he was proud of me. On our last night together, he told me he was proud of me. As I look back, I feel like he made sure that he said whatever needed to be said to others during those last days. I really treasure that one statement that I heard from my father on our last night together. "I'm proud of you."

5. **Prepare your loved ones.** During my last night with my dad, he said to me, "You have pulled yourself up by your own boot straps and become a great lady."

I remember thinking, "Pulled myself up by my own boot straps? I have had such a wonderful husband, such a wonderful church, and such wonderful parents. Why did he say, 'by my own boot straps'?"

When I missed my dad in the days and months to come, I often thought of those words, "by your own boot straps." When I missed my husband as he became busy with his new duties as pastor, I thought of those words, "by your own boot straps." When I became discouraged, I exhorted myself, "Now is the time to pull yourself up by your own boot straps and be a great lady." My dad's last words to me on this earth prepared me for the future.

Soon my dad's supper was finished. He couldn't eat as much as he used to eat. A nurse entered the room and told me I should leave for a while. Dad needed some rest because he had a big day of surgery scheduled for the next day.

"Dad," I asked before I left, "would you like me to come back and check on you every hour?"

"Please check on me every 30 minutes," he replied, "and wake me up when Jack gets here. I need to talk to him." (My husband stayed with my dad during the night, and I went home until the morning.)

I checked on Dad every 30 minutes. He was asleep almost every time I checked on him. We spoke very little after that. Just once he said groggily, "Don't forget to have Jack come in when he gets here."

My husband arrived. I told him Dad wanted to talk to him, and I left for home. I would never again speak alone with my Dad on this earth. But I left feeling needed and important. I left with his blessing and the words I would need to carry me through the days ahead.

The following January I changed the flowers on my dad's crypt. I drove away and thought to myself, "That's all I can do for my father now—put those flowers on his crypt. That doesn't benefit Dad. I'm really doing it for myself."

I drove toward Hyles-Anderson College to go to work at the Christian Womanhood Office. As I pulled into the driveway of the college, I thought, "That's okay, Cindy. You did all you could when he was alive. That's what is important." I headed in to work. "I have no regrets," I thought.

For those of you who have a wonderful father like mine, I congratulate you! If he is on this earth, don't forget to wait on him and to make him feel loved and needed. Don't forget to tell him you are proud he is your father. Say what needs to be said. Don't forget to say "thank you" and to laugh with him a bit.

If your father, like mine, waits for you in Heaven, don't forget to remember and be thankful for a godly father. Then pull yourself up by your own boot straps and have a great day!

6

How My Grandmother, Coystal Mattie Hyles, Influenced Me

So often when I am confused or have a tough question, I look back on my godly heritage, and my questions are answered. In fact, I believe it is since the death of Mamaw Hyles that her life has taught me my greatest lesson.

As I was thinking of her life, a thought really startled me. My grandmother was married to an alcoholic who abused her physically, and she lived in extreme poverty. (She was not exactly the kind of daughter of whom one would be proud.) She also lost two daughters in death. Actually, her life was full of failure and sorrow until my dad's ministry began to flourish.

The amazing thing to me is that my grandmother was 68 years old before she knew any success in life. This is the age she was when my dad's ministry at Miller Road Baptist Church in Garland, Texas, began to "take off." Coystal Mattie Hyles is now recognized by many to be one of the most successful mothers in the history of Christendom. My dad and my aunt, Earlyne Stephens, have been a great credit to her name.

The following are some of the lessons we can learn as a result of this thought.

1. Be patient with others even when they disappoint us time and again. Perhaps our friend's children are making straight A's while our children go from failure to failure. We may be tempted to throw up our hands and say, "They will never amount to anything."

Maybe we know an adult friend or loved one who is not living for the Lord. We're tempted to say, "Why keep praying? Her life is already wasted." How shortsighted we must seem to God!

2. Be patient with ourselves and God's leading in our lives even when it seems we are seeing few successes. I wonder if my Great-Grandfather Frasure ever said, "My daughter's married to an alcoholic. Where did I go wrong as a parent?" He probably didn't know that he had a part in one of God's choicest designs.

I am so glad we only need to follow the Lord day by day and don't need to be concerned with the degree of greatness we have achieved or what others may think of our accomplishments.

3. Be careful about criticizing others when they fail. I imagine the critics of my grandmother's day may have said something like this: "Look how that Frasure girl turned out. Her parents probably didn't spend enough time with her." How grieved the Lord must be when we hurl cruel words toward His unfinished masterpieces. I'm grateful that the Lord sees the total picture of our lives.

I am also thankful for a grandmother who never gave up. Through her perseverance, she has been able to influence my life—even after her death. Reflecting on her life continues to open doors and turn on lights for me.

CONCLUSION

Genesis 44:30c, 44:34a, *"….seeing that his life is bound up in the lad's life….For how shall I go up to my father, and the lad be not with me?"*

Excuse me as I am taking these verses out of context. This is really talking about Judah's not wanting to go back to his father Jacob without his younger brother Benjamin's being with him. But I have these verses underlined in my Bible with the names "Jaclynn" and "Kenny" beside them.

While I was rearing our children, my life was bound up in their lives. My supreme desires were these:

1. I wanted God to use my husband.
2. I wanted our children to turn out right and to do God's will.

I did not want to see Jesus in Heaven without our children's being saved and going with me. I did not want to serve the Lord but leave our children behind in the world.

My prayer is that something you as a reader have read in this book will cause you to bind up your life in the Lord, your husband, and your children.

My prayer is that you will learn from this book how to be sure that your children are not only saved, but also that they are living as kings and queens by serving the King of Kings. My prayer is that none of us will go up to the Father without our children.

Appendix A

Commandments and Promises for Child Rearing

Exodus 20:5
"Thou shalt not bow down thyself to them, nor serve them: for I the LORD thy God am a jealous God, visiting the iniquity of the fathers upon the children unto the third and fourth generation of them that hate me."

Numbers 14:18
"The LORD is longsuffering, and of great mercy, forgiving iniquity and transgression, and by no means clearing the guilty, visiting the iniquity of the fathers upon the children unto the third and fourth generation."

Deuteronomy 4:40
*"Thou shalt keep therefore his statutes, and his commandments, which I command thee this day, **that it may go well with thee, and with thy children after thee,** and that thou mayest prolong thy days upon the earth, which the LORD thy God giveth thee, for ever."*

Deuteronomy 5:9
"Thou shalt not bow down thyself unto them, nor serve them: for I the LORD thy God am a jealous God, visiting the iniquity of the fathers upon the children unto the third and fourth generation of them that hate me."

Deuteronomy 5:29

"O that there were such an heart in them, that they would fear me, and keep all my commandments always, that it might be well with them, and with their children for ever!"

Deuteronomy 11:19-21

*"**And ye shall teach them your children**, speaking of them when thou sittest in thine house, and when thou walkest by the way, when thou liest down, and when thou risest up. And thou shalt write them upon the door posts of thine house, and upon thy gates: **That your days may be multiplied, and the days of your children**, in the land which the LORD sware unto your fathers to give them, as the days of heaven upon the earth."*

Deuteronomy 12:28

"Observe and hear all these words which I command thee, that it may go well with thee, and with thy children after thee for ever, when thou doest that which is good and right in the sight of the LORD thy God."

Deuteronomy 28:1-4

*"And it shall come to pass, if thou shalt hearken diligently unto the voice of the LORD thy God, to observe and to do all his commandments which I command thee this day, that the LORD thy God will set thee on high above all nations of the earth: And all these blessings shall come on thee, and overtake thee, if thou shalt hearken unto the voice of the LORD thy God. Blessed shalt thou be in the city, and blessed shalt thou be in the field. **Blessed shall be the fruit of thy body,** and the fruit of thy ground, and the fruit of thy cattle, the increase of thy kine, and the flocks of thy sheep."*

Deuteronomy 31:12

"Gather the people together, men, and women, and children, and thy stranger that is within thy gates, that they may hear, and that they may learn, and fear the LORD your God, and observe to do all the words of this law."

Deuteronomy 32:46, 47

*"And he said unto them, Set your hearts unto all the words which I testify among you this day, **which ye shall command your children to observe***

to do, all the words of this law. For it is not a vain thing for you; because it is your life: and through this thing ye shall prolong your days in the land, whither ye go over Jordan to possess it."

Joshua 4:19-24

"And the people came up out of Jordan on the tenth day of the first month, and encamped in Gilgal, in the east border of Jericho. And those twelve stones, which they took out of Jordan, did Joshua pitch in Gilgal. And he spake unto the children of Israel, saying, **When your children shall ask their fathers in time to come, saying, What mean these stones? Then ye shall let your children know,** saying, Israel came over this Jordan on dry land. For the LORD your God dried up the waters of Jordan from before you, until ye were passed over, as the LORD your God did to the Red sea, which he dried up from before us, until we were gone over: That all the people of the earth might know the hand of the LORD, that it is mighty: that ye might fear the LORD your God for ever."

Joshua 14:9

"And Moses sware on that day, saying, **Surely the land whereon thy feet have trodden shall be thine inheritance, and thy children's for ever, because thou hast wholly followed the LORD my God.**"

I Samuel 3:13

"For I have told him that I will judge his house for ever for the iniquity which he knoweth; because his sons made themselves vile, and he restrained them not."

II Samuel 7:29

"Therefore now let it please thee to bless the house of thy servant, that it may continue for ever before thee: for thou, O Lord GOD, hast spoken it: and with thy blessing **let the house of thy servant be blessed for ever.**"

I Kings 15:3-5

"And he walked in all the sins of his father, which he had done before him: and his heart was not perfect with the LORD his God, as the heart of David *his father.* **Nevertheless for David's sake did the L**ORD **his God give him a lamp in Jerusalem, to set up his son after him,** *and to establish Jerusalem:* **Because David did that which was right in the eyes of the L**ORD**, and turned not aside from any thing that he commanded him all the days of his life,** *save only in the matter of Uriah the Hittite."*

I Chronicles 28:8

*"Now therefore in the sight of all Israel the congregation of the L*ORD*, and in the audience of our God, keep and seek for all the commandments of the L*ORD *your God:* **that ye may possess this good land, and leave it for an inheritance for your children after you for ever.***"*

Ezra 9:12

"Now therefore give not your daughters unto their sons, neither take their daughters unto your sons, nor seek their peace or their wealth for ever: that ye may be strong, and eat the good of the land, and leave it for an inheritance to your children for ever."

Psalm 22:30, 31

*"A seed shall serve him; it shall be accounted to the L*ORD *for a generation. They shall come, and shall declare his righteousness unto a people that shall be born, that he hath done this."*

Psalm 48:13

"Mark ye well her bulwarks, consider her palaces; that ye may tell it to the generation following."

Psalm 79:13

"So we thy people and sheep of thy pasture will give thee thanks for ever: we will shew forth thy praise to all generations."

Psalm 102:18

"This shall be written for the generation to come: and the people which shall be created shall praise the Lord."

Psalm 102:28

"The children of thy servants shall continue, and their seed shall be established before thee."

Psalm 103:17, 18

"But the mercy of the LORD is from everlasting to everlasting upon them that fear him, and his righteousness unto children's children; To such as keep his covenant, and to those that remember his commandments to do them."

Psalm 112:1, 2

"Praise ye the LORD. Blessed is the man that feareth the LORD, that delighteth greatly in his commandments. His seed shall be mighty upon earth: the generation of the upright shall be blessed."

Psalm 115:14

"The LORD shall increase you more and more, you and your children."

Psalm 145:4

"One generation shall praise thy works to another, and shall declare thy mighty acts."

Psalm 147:13

"For he hath strengthened the bars of thy gates; he hath blessed thy children within thee."

Proverbs 13:22

"A good man leaveth an inheritance to his children's children: and the wealth of the sinner is laid up for the just."

Proverbs 19:13a

"A foolish son is the calamity of his father...."

Proverbs 20:7

"The just man walketh in his integrity: his children are blessed after him."

Proverbs 20:11

"Even a child is known by his doings, whether his work be pure, and whether it be right."

Proverbs 22:6

"Train up a child in the way he should go: and when he is old, he will not depart from it."

Proverbs 23:24

"The father of the righteous shall greatly rejoice: and he that begetteth a wise child shall have joy of him."

Proverbs 23:26

"My son, give me thine heart, and let thine eyes observe my ways."

Proverbs 31:1-9

"The words of king Lemuel, the prophecy that his mother taught him. What, my son? and what, the son of my womb? and what, the son of my vows? Give not thy strength unto women, nor thy ways to that which destroyeth kings. It is not for kings, O Lemuel, it is not for kings to drink wine; nor for princes strong drink: Lest they drink, and forget the law, and pervert the judgment of any of the afflicted. Give strong drink unto him that is ready to perish, and wine unto those that be of heavy hearts. Let him drink, and forget his poverty, and remember his misery no more. Open thy mouth for the dumb in the cause of all such as are appointed to destruction. Open thy mouth, judge righteously, and plead the cause of the poor and needy."

Proverbs 31:21

"She is not afraid of the snow for her household: for all her household are clothed with scarlet."

Proverbs 31:27

"She looketh well to the ways of her household, and eateth not the bread of idleness."

Proverbs 31:28

"Her children arise up, and call her blessed; her husband also, and he praiseth her."

Isaiah 8:16-18

"Bind up the testimony, seal the law among my disciples. And I will wait upon the LORD, that hideth his face from the house of Jacob, and I will look for him. Behold, I and the children whom the LORD hath given me are for signs and for wonders in Israel from the LORD of hosts which dwelleth in Mount Zion."

Isaiah 48:17-19

"Thus saith the LORD, thy Redeemer, the Holy One of Israel; I am the LORD thy God which teacheth thee to profit, which leadeth thee by the way that thou shouldest go. O that thou hadst hearkened to my commandments! then had thy peace been as a river and thy righteousness as the waves of the sea: Thy **seed** also had been as the sand, and the offspring of thy bowels like the gravel thereof; his name should not have been cut off nor destroyed from before me.

Isaiah 49:25

"But thus saith the LORD, Even the captives of the mighty shall be taken away, and the prey of the terrible shall be delivered: for I will contend with him that contendeth with thee, and I will save thy children."

Isaiah 54:13, 14a

"And all thy children shall be taught of the LORD; and great shall be the peace of thy children. In righteousness shalt thou be established."

Isaiah 58:12

"And they that shall be of thee shall build the old waste places: thou shalt raise up the foundations of many generations; and thou shalt be called, The repairer of the breach, The restorer of paths to dwell in."

Isaiah 59:21

"As for me, this is my covenant with them, saith the LORD; My spirit that is upon thee, and my words which I have put in thy mouth, shall not depart out of thy mouth, nor out of the mouth of thy seed, nor out of the mouth of thy seed's seed, saith the LORD, from henceforth and for ever."

Jeremiah 32:38, 39

"And they shall be my people, and I will be their God: And I will give them one heart, and one way, that they may fear me for ever, for the good of them, and of their children after them."

Job 5:25

"Thou shalt know also that thy seed shall be great, and thine offspring as the grass of the earth."

Matthew 7:11

"If ye then, being evil, know how to give good gifts unto your children, how much more shall your Father which is in heaven give good things to them that ask him?"

Appendix B

THE SCHAAP FAMILY

D r. and Mrs. Jack Schaap are the parents of two children. They have two grandchildren.

Jack Allan Schaap . . . . .October 1, 1957
Cindy Lynn Hyles Schaap . . . . .November 30, 1959

  Jaclynn April Schaap Weber .April 16, 1981
  Todd Andrew Weber . . . . .October 21, 1980
    Lyndsay Alana Weber . . . . .March 18, 2005
    Raymond Jack Weber . . . . .August 19, 2006

  Kenneth Jack Frasure Schaap . . . . .November 14, 1984
  Candace Janel Hooker Schaap . . . . .September 27, 1984

The Schaap Family

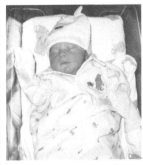

Raymond Jack Weber